David
II.

Splendor from the Sea
As a Tree Grows
Bold under God—A Fond Look at a Frontier Preacher
A Shepherd Looks at Psalm 23
A Layman Looks at the Lord's Prayer
Rabboni—Which Is to Say, Master
A Shepherd Looks at the Good Shepherd and His Sheep
A Gardener Looks at the Fruits of the Spirit
Mighty Man of Valor—Gideon
Mountain Splendor
Taming Tension
Expendable
Still Waters
A Child Looks at Psalm 23
Ocean Glory
Walking with God
On Wilderness Trails
Elijah—Prophet of Power
Salt for Society
A Layman Looks at the Lamb of God
Lessons from a Sheep Dog
Wonder o' the Wind
Joshua—Man of Fearless Faith
A Layman Looks at the Love of God
Sea Edge
Chosen Vessels
David I

W. Phillip Keller

David

The Shepherd King

WORD BOOKS
PUBLISHER
WACO, TEXAS

A DIVISION OF
WORD, INCORPORATED

Library of Congress Cataloging-in-Publication Data
(Revised for vol. 2)

Keller, W. Phillip (Weldon Phillip), 1920–
    David.

    Contents: 1. The time of Saul's tyranny—2. The shepherd king.
    1. David, King of Israel.   2. Saul, King of Israel.
3. Jews—Kings and rulers—Biography. 4. Bible. O.T.
Biography. I. Title.
BS580.D3K43 1985   222'.40924   85–6265
ISBN 0–8499–0470–6 (v. 1)
ISBN 0–8499–0559–1 (v. 2)

Printed in the United States of America

67898   BKC   987654321

To
Miss Muriel Perrott of Great Britain
and
Miss Ruth Truesdell of the United States.

Both were my early teachers in Africa. They instilled in this rough, young, frontier lad a great love for fine literature and a most profound respect for God's Word.

In Appreciation

First of all, my genuine gratitude is given to God for sufficient strength and stamina to complete this work. It extended over a four-year period of time. His presence, by His Spirit, was manifest in every area of the endeavor. More often than not the impression which came to me was that I was but the scribe, He was the author.

My sincere thanks go to the various churches, both in California and Canada, which opened their doors and offered their facilities for the studies. The loyalty of some of their people touched me deeply. Some traveled seventy miles to attend the sessions every week.

It was a special joy to have Ursula, my wife, assist me again in typing the manuscript with such precision. Through our Father's tender care, her health was restored so she could share in the project.

Finally, I am deeply grateful to the men and women in different places who made tapes of the studies, who took care of the sanctuaries, who gave so generously of their time, and who prayed faithfully for all of us.

Blessings! Best wishes.

Contents

Author's Introductory Note

It is important for the reader of this book to realize that this is the second volume dealing with David's life. The first covered his career up until the end of Saul's rule of tyranny. This second volume recounts the building of David's empire up to the time of Solomon's rule.

It must be repeated here that this work is not just a historical narrative. Rather, it is a devotional study showing what our Father can do with an individual, who, above all else, is determined to do God's will. It must be borne in mind that David was a man of strengths and weaknesses, of light and darkness, of passion and piety—just as we are.

This book does not attempt either to exalt the man or to vilify him. It endeavors to portray David exactly as he is depicted for us by the Spirit of God in Scripture. My main concern has been to show, in layman's language, what it is God can achieve with anyone open and available to His purposes. Thereby it is my earnest hope readers everywhere would be challenged to give themselves fully to the Most High in a genuine outpouring of loyalty and love.

Every effort has been made to keep the record in simple chronological order. In this, author's license has been used. This work has been shared with study groups throughout the country. In those sessions the Lord has been pleased to speak to His people in profound, life-changing ways. He can do the same for anyone who reads these pages with a humble, receptive spirit, open to His Word.

My sincere prayer is, this will happen.

W. Phillip Keller

David
II.

1

David Becomes King of Judah

The tragic death of Saul and his three sons, Jonathan, Abinadab and Melchishua, the princes of Israel, marked the end of the era of Saul's terrible tyranny. In a single day, under the furious attack of the Philistine archers, all four men fell in combat on the slopes of Mount Gilboa. It was as though the door had suddenly been slammed shut on the disastrous dynasty of Israel's first monarch.

The nation as a whole, after forty years of Saul's despicable leadership, lay shattered and prostrate beneath the iron heel of the enemy Philistines. The ruthless invaders now occupied many of the most lovely towns. Their power and control had taken over most of the territory formerly governed by Saul. So Israel now suffered as a people torn by war and beaten down in battle.

At this low point of despair, David, still resident at Ziklag, sensed that the hour had come when he should return from his long exile among the Philistines. He knew, of course, that it was within the divine purposes of God that eventually he should be the one to restore Israel to a position of power. He had been anointed by

Samuel to this end. He had been quietly reassured by Jonathan, his dearest friend, it would happen in due course. For seven, long, dreadful years, he had lived in terror under attack from Saul. At last the agony of his exile was behind him.

If Israel was to be forged into a mighty empire under the hand of God, it would call for remarkable leadership. That leadership would have to come from David. For at this point in her horrendous history, the nation had no other noble leader. Any who might have aspired to the role were either weak in character or cunning in personal ambition.

Not only would David have to overcome the rivalry and chicanery of other contenders for the nation's throne, but also he would have the formidable challenge of uniting the people into a single unit. Deep divisions had arisen between the followers of Saul, most of whom came from the ten tribes of Israel, and those who were loyal to David, drawn mainly from the powerful tribe of Judah. In a sense, the nation, broken in battle by the Philistines, also lay shattered by the internal strife between its own rival camps.

Perhaps at no time in history was any man confronted with a greater challenge to create a vast world power out of such unpromising material. It was worse than starting from a small handful of despondent people. It meant mending grievous old wounds and bitter hostilities that otherwise could cripple any attempts to build an empire of power in the Middle East.

With his deep spiritual perception, David could see all of this clearly. Therefore, he was wise enough to realize that only clear direction from the Lord would enable him to begin the restoration of the nation. To this end he inquired of God whether in fact this was now the appropriate time for him to return to reside in Judah.

David sensed that his painful years of exile among the enemy Philistines were over. But precisely where should he go? What city should he choose for his new headquarters in Judah? There was no doubt in his mind he should return home. But much more specifically, he was determined to live only where God ordained he should live. It might be assumed that Bethlehem, the village where he had grown up and which he knew so well, would be a logical choice. But it was not the place of Jehovah's appointment. Rather, David was directed to Hebron.

On the surface this might seem an insignificant matter. Yet in truth and in principle it was momentous. For it demonstrated that David was making a significant shift in his recent mode of life. Instead of being headstrong and self-assertive in carrying out his own schemes, he was willing here to seek to do the will of the Most High. This was true both in a general way and, even more importantly, in the specific details of his decisions.

It was not enough just to know God wanted him to go back up to Judah. David took great pains to be sure that Hebron was where he would live for the next seven years.

As God's people, we need to be as precise and careful in seeking the counsel of Christ for the decisions we make. Not only will His gracious Spirit guide us in general ways, but also in the minute details of our decisions, if we will patiently seek His will and comply with His wishes. Many of us miss the exhilaration of enjoying the constant company of Christ simply because we do not consider it critical to determine the desires of His heart for us in the details of life. He delights to have us move in quiet harmony with Him.

This David was discovering.

So when he and his followers moved to Hebron, great and exciting events began to occur. It was the precise place of God's appointment for David. And it was there he would begin to see God's astonishing arrangement of his affairs.

Hebron was a center noteworthy in the history of Israel. It was the first place in Palestine to be actually acquired by Abraham as a possession in the land of promise. Here he purchased a large tract of ground known as the field of Machpelah, where he buried Sarah with great honor. Some four hundred years later, it was reoccupied by Joshua when he invaded the land of Canaan. Later Caleb claimed it as his inheritance.

Hebron was famous for the Anakim giants who once held the region as their mountain stronghold. With all of its proud traditions, this is the spot where David was to reestablish himself among the people of Judah.

Here he brought his two wives. Ahinoam came from the northern plains of Jezreel. The beautiful Abigail came from the southern hill country of Carmel. If the two women, drawn from the diverse regions and tribes of the nation, could live in harmony within his household, David no doubt felt confident the twelve tribes could eventually live in peace under his monarchy. At least it was a good omen for the future.

Here, too, at Hebron, David settled all the six hundred fighting men who had followed him into exile. He brought their families to live with them, forming a formidable nucleus of loyal citizens who would act as ambassadors of good will to the rest of Judah.

It will be remembered that David had always been astute enough to cultivate the favor of his fellow tribesmen from Judah during his daring exploits as an exile. He would restore the livestock and loot plundered from them by the Philistines and the Amalekites. He would send them generous gifts of booty gathered up in his own dashing raids. He would spare and guard their flocks and herds whenever he came across them in his campaigns.

So it was not surprising that in short order the leaders and patriarchs of Judah decided that David deserved to be made their monarch. No explicit details have been given regarding this coronation ceremony. One can only conclude that it was carried out with the utmost integrity and sincerity of purpose. Judah desperately needed a bold and brilliant leader. The consensus of their choice was to anoint David as king.

The first noble action David undertook as king was to dispatch a delegation to Jabesh-gilead, across the Jordan, commending them for the tribute they bestowed on Saul's household by giving Saul and his sons an honorable burial. The Philistines, after slaughtering the king of Israel and his three princes on Mount Gilboa, had taken the four corpses and hung them in disgrace upon the walls of the city of Bethshan. It was a despicable deed.

With incredible courage, brave warriors from Jabesh-gilead had made a night march across country. Taking down the decomposing corpses, they carried them home. The bodies were cremated, then given honorable burial in their own desert sands. It was a heroic gesture of gratitude for the deliverance Saul had brought them when under attack from the Ammonites who had threatened to enslave them.

David, in commending them for this brave and noble action, demonstrated again his own enormous capacity to forgive those who had wronged him. Despite the cruel harassment he had suffered at Saul's hands for so many years, David was prepared to overlook those injustices

19

and give honor to the king first chosen to rule his people.

This ability to be big enough to be compassionate to those who opposed him stands out boldly as one of the great strengths of David's character. He did it with his older brothers who maligned him. He did it with Achish who called him "a madman." He did it with Nabal who insulted him. And because of it God, in every instance, brought blessing and benefits to him for his splendid behavior.

This capacity to forgive was proof positive that David had, in truth, known and experienced the forgiveness of God for his own failings. It needs to be added here that any Christian who claims the forgiveness of Christ for his or her own wrongs, but refuses to forgive another, is indulging in self-delusion. Once we taste the emancipation of our Father's forgiveness, we cannot, we will not, withhold it from our fellows. We are glad to forgive!

David also used the occasion to announce to the tribes of Israel that the tribe of Judah had anointed him to be their king. Perhaps he hoped this diplomatic gesture would also generate some good will from his erstwhile rivals.

But it was not to be. General Abner, the fierce and formidable commander of Saul's forces—who by the way had succeeded David in this position—was determined that Saul's dynasty should survive. In part this can be understood since he was Saul's cousin, and also because it would preserve his own power and perhaps give him a chance in due course to usurp the throne.

Still, it was a dangerous course upon which he set himself. He knew full well that Samuel had long ago anointed David to replace Saul as king over all of Israel. He knew God had rejected Saul and his family from the monarchy. He knew it was inevitable the purposes of God would be fulfilled. Still in dogged stubbornness, he chose to ensconce Ishbosheth, Saul's only surviving son, as sovereign in his father's stead.

Ishbosheth was a weakling. His very name means, "man of shame," or, even worse, "man of Baal." But he was one whom Abner could manipulate and readily use for his own nefarious ends.

For David the decision to do this was somewhat frustrating. It meant the nation was clearly divided into two rival monarchies. He would have to wait years for reunification to take place, while any hope he had of starting to build a great empire under God's good hand would have to be deferred.

About this time David composed Psalm 27. In it he gives moving expression to his unflinching faith in the Lord. Only He could sustain him in his frustration. He alone could guide him through the unknown future. It would be Jehovah who would deliver him from his enemies.

In stark reality, amidst all of its defeat, the entire nation stood on the brink of civil war. Only the self-restraint and quiet composure of David saved his people from great peril. Abner, on the other hand, regrouped his forces and used the quiet interlude to recover much of the northern regions from the oppression and ravages of the Philistines.

So bit by bit, year upon year, Abner managed to consolidate the northern kingdom. He brought all the regions of Gilead, Ashur, Jezreel, Ephraim and Benjamin, as well as the rest of Israel, under the monarchy of Ishbosheth. His royal residence was set up in Mahanaim, across the Jordan, roughly fifty miles from Hebron.

As it turned out later, the hapless king would only rule here for two short years. His end would be tragic and sudden, cut short in the providential purposes of the Almighty.

Abner, having established his influence over Israel by military power, now set his sights on seizing the region of Judah. This was not presumptuous, for he commanded a powerful army of nearly one third of a million men. David, on the other hand, had come out of exile with a small, tough band of six hundred battle-hardened raiders.

Abner's first foray across the southern reaches of the Jordan brought him to the beautiful pool at Gibeon. Gibeon at this point in Israel's murky history was where the sacred tabernacle and its precious Ark of the Covenant were ensconced. They had been moved there from Nob after Saul in his demented fury slaughtered eighty-five of the priests of the Lord.

Perhaps it was felt the sanctuary of the Most High would be safer in this southern community. Also it would be easier for the Gibeonites, made slaves by Joshua to serve the Levites, to provide wood and water in this place.

There is no question that David knew all about Abner's ambitions for power. He had informants all across the Judean hills and valleys who now alerted him to Abner's movements. So when the Israeli general came to Gibeon, he was confronted at once by a contingent of David's finest fighting men. Among them were three of David's own nephews, all sons of Zeruiah, David's sister—Joab, Abishai and Asahel. Of these Joab had become David's commanding officer, Abner's exact counterpart. Abishai was the fearless young lion who had accompanied David into the very center of Saul's night camp and begged leave to plunge his spear through the sleeping monarch's chest. Asahel was a marvelous athlete, swift as a gazelle, eager for war.

Of the three Joab was by far the most formidable warrior. There was about him a rugged loyalty to David that could not be denied. Yet he was a ruthless killer who seemed destitute of any spiritual values. He was cunning, determined, worldly wise, vindictive and quick to act to advance the power and prestige of his monarch. On the one hand, he achieved astonishing exploits for David. On the other, he brought the king agonizing remorse to the end of his life.

Joab and Abner now confronted each other across the placid pool. It was such a peaceful spot, a bit like Geneva, where the issues of war and conquest would be decided. Men, even at their best, are still butchers. And the unregenerate soul thinks only in terms of blood shed and battles won. And since neither Abner or Joab were men of God, they saw no wrong in settling their differences with a bit of grisly swordplay between their young champions. What were a handful of lives forfeited for "fun"?

Men were expendable! Life was cheap! Get on with the games! Let's see who survives!

It was a sinister replay of the epic when Goliath stormed up and down the banks of the Valley of Blood, challenging any Hebrew youth to cross the stream and do battle in hand-to-hand combat. In those desperate days, only David dared to attack the giant Anakim. Now again a dozen of Abner's toughest tigers stepped forward to challenge the men of Judah.

Combat-hardened from years of desert raids under David's fierce command, twelve of Joab's young lions leaped to the attack, eager for slaughter. In brutal, bestial hand-to-hand struggle, all the warriors plunged their cruel swords into each other. The struggle erupted into a full-scale battle with enormous losses to Abner and his men.

What had begun as a game escalated into a massacre. By nightfall three hundred and eighty gallant men lay dead across the southern desert. Twenty of them were from Judah. The others were the terror-stricken warriors from Israel. It had been a ghastly rout for Abner.

In dismay and astonishment, he, too, fled for his life. But young Asahel, Joab's fleet-footed brother, pursued him relentlessly. If David would not let him destroy Saul, no one would stop him from plunging his spear through Abner.

Abner looked back and warned Asahel to relent. But the young man was bent on blood. Suddenly in midstride, the wily Abner stopped, plunged the point of his spear beneath the young man's ribs and so provided Asahel with a gory spike on which he impaled himself. His rash and stubborn refusal to heed Abner's repeated warnings cost him his life. Even more alarming, it would also cost Abner his, since Joab would avenge his brother's death.

He and Abishai went in hot pursuit of Abner. But he eluded them and by dark had taken his stand on a hill where his men rallied around him. From there he shouted to Joab that they should call a truce. Why should the fray be allowed to erupt into a full-scale civil war between brothers? The sword would go on taking its awful toll and the end would be appalling bitterness for their people.

Fortunately the infuriated Joab allowed reason to prevail over his passion for blind revenge. He had the trumpet blown to call a halt to the slaughter, knowing full well that somehow, somewhere, very soon he would see to it that Abner paid the ultimate price for his deeds.

That night both sides withdrew from Gibeon. They had come to a place of peace and left it stained dark with blackened blood of nearly four hundred young fighters. It was an atrocious cost that had to be met in order for the two commanders to see what a civil war would and could mean in loss of life.

Abner and his troops withdrew across the Jordan and returned to Mahanaim. Joab and his triumphant forces retired back to Hebron. Asahel was given an honorable burial in Bethlehem, his home village, where David, too, had grown up as a lad.

There is a profound lesson here for God's people. We simply cannot allow personal pride, ambition and the quest for power to dominate our desires. Those in the world are always inclined "to play their games." The urge to use cunning, political advantage, and personal influence to advance one's selfish ends is very much a part of the social scene.

It should not be so for the Christian!

To do so can cost both us and others enormous losses. We can be consumed by our own dreadful desires. And what began as a game can end in the gall of bitterness!

2

Abner Defects to David

The seven long years that David waited in Hebron for the unification of the nation must have seemed to him more like seventy. Though his personal power and influence and popularity with his people increased steadily, while that of Ishbosheth waned, there still stood in his way the intransigence of Abner. The brilliant general exploited every opportunity that came his way to consolidate his grip and dominance over Israel.

Abner had long been David's deadly rival. From the dramatic day in which David slew Goliath, the cunning commander had treated David with disdain. Saul had asked him then who David was and he feigned ignorance even though they both came from the same community of Bethlehem. Later Abner was supplanted by David as commander by Saul because of the youth's heroic exploits. In his demented state Saul later demoted David and replaced him with Abner. Then, ultimately, when David fled into exile in the wilderness it was Abner who hunted him relentlessly "like a partridge in the hills," with a formidable force of 3,000 picked men.

Abner Defects to David

Now that Saul had perished, Abner used all the military advantage and political power at his command to thwart David's legitimate rise to the position of national king. Even though Abner conducted a protracted and bloody campaign against David it was bound to fail for in truth it was against the purposes of God for His people. This David had to believe in quiet faith. He had to trust God to do His own unique work behind the scenes to resolve the impossible impasse between the two rivals. At times it must have looked hopeless as Abner became stronger and stronger in Israel.

The Word of God makes it very clear to us that all who come to power in any area of human society do so only by the permissive will and purposes of God. It follows then that men and women rise or fall according to His wish.

Few of us truly believe this. David did. He was confident that in His own good time Jehovah God would establish his kingdom in the nation and empower him to rule God's people both politically as a statesman and spiritually as a shepherd. This was God's covenant with him. He would carry it out.

As Christians living in the late twentieth century, we would do well to trust God in the same way. He it is who brings leaders to power in His own sovereign might. And we need to entreat Him earnestly not only for our own leaders, but for all those throughout all nations who hold sway over their fellows. This applies not only in the realm of politics, but also in business, in the church, in the media, in education and in science. Our God is able to work wonders behind the scenes, screened from our human view, if we will but trust Him.

This David did, without flinching, in quiet faith. The

results were dramatic and astonishing beyond his wildest dreams.

Suddenly there was a deep rupture in the relationship between Ishbosheth and Abner. The weak and impotent king charged Abner with having an illicit affair with Rizpah, one of Saul's concubines. This may or may not have been a true accusation. Abner may very well have overstepped the bounds of propriety in his heady rise to power. If so, it was indeed a dangerous move, because to claim one of the king's concubines was tantamount to claiming the entire harem, and therefore the throne. So Ishbosheth could have felt threatened by this action.

In any case, the charge so enraged Abner that in a fit of unbridled fury he turned against the monarch he himself had put on the throne. He swore that he would switch his allegiance from the dynasty of Saul and offer the entire ten tribes to David, the king of Judah. After all, he knew this to be God's will!

It was a drastic turn-about of astonishing proportions!

The weak-kneed Ishbosheth simply trembled at the terrifying consequences. For him it was the end of his rule. There was nothing he could do or say to deter his angry general.

Without waiting to reconsider the end results of his drastic decisions, Abner dispatched messengers to David. The news they brought was astonishing and almost beyond belief. Suddenly David's entrenched rival, so powerful in Israel, was offering to form an alliance with him. For certain considerations, Abner suggested that they form a league whereby he would use his own immense influence to bring all of Israel over to David.

No doubt a part of the deal would be that Abner would be elevated to the powerful position of commander-in-chief of all of David's forces. This would seem natural if he brought with him the huge standing army now under his command. But it certainly would not sit well with Joab, whose smaller force had already shown its superiority in battle.

David's response to Abner's overture of peace was immediate. He would be glad to meet the man. He would certainly consider such a league. Yet there remained one absolute condition that must first be met. It seemed strange indeed in the midst of such important military matters. David simply refused to see Abner unless he brought with him Saul's daughter, Michal, his long estranged wife, the beautiful girl for whose hand he had risked his own life in slaughtering two hundred Philistines fourteen years before.

When Michal refused to go into exile with David and chose instead to remain at home with her own royal family of Saul's household, the results were diabolical. Saul, as an insult to David, gave her to another man, Phaltiel by name. Now she would be torn away from him and, under direct orders from Abner, be brought back to David. Strange as it may seem, the parting was much more painful for Phaltiel, who accompanied her as far as Bahurim, than it was for Michal. She was a tough lady who seemed incapable of showing great love or devotion to any man.

In any event, she would now be the seventh wife in David's ever-increasing harem. And since she was childless, her rank in the hierarchy would not be that of "first lady" by any measurement. Still as a point of pride David demanded her return. If nothing else, it would be a diplomatic move that helped to consolidate his kingship in reuniting his household with that of Saul from the kingdom of Israel.

It is noteworthy that each of David's other wives bore him a son. Of these Amnon was the eldest, Cheleab (also called Dan) the second in succession, and Absalom the third, followed by Adonijah the fourth in line, with others in descending order of rank.

David would live to rue the marriage alliance he made with some of these women. Their sons and offspring born to him would bring him never-ending grief and painful sorrow to the twilight of his life. Especially in marrying Maacah, a pagan princess from Geshur, he had contravened God's explicit commands to Israel never to wed a heathen woman. Her vile and vicious son, Absalom, would eventually murder his elder brother Amnon, then rise up in rebellion against David to usurp the throne of his very own father (see Joshua 23:11–13).

Again the basic spiritual principle here is that inevitably in life one reaps what one sows. The clear commandments of the Most High cannot be contravened at will without paying the calamitous consequences. The ordinances of the Lord are established for the benefit and well-being of His people. Those who comply with His wishes are blessed and enriched. Those who despise His edicts and disobey His will suffer. David did!

Before coming to Hebron to meet with David, Abner took the trouble to confer with the elders of Israel. In a unique and intuitive way, the cunning commander was well aware that the nation's leaders had long wished for David to become their monarch. They had known this was God's intention for them as a people. Nor had they forgotten those tempestuous times when the aged Samuel had declared fearlessly to Saul that because of his deliberate disobedience to the edict of Jehovah to wipe out the Amalekites, he and his family were rejected from reigning in Israel.

Abner Defects to David

Despite all his devious devices to try and perpetuate this family in power, Abner, in personal revenge against Ishbosheth, now called on the elders of Israel to give their full allegiance to David. The sudden about-face must have startled them, but Abner, to cushion the shock, resorted to spiritual truth to win them over.

He reminded them that it was the Most High God who had promised to bring the nation to great power through David. It was King David who would deliver them not only from the Philistines, but also from all their ancient enemies surrounding them on all sides. So why not act now? Why not form an alliance with Judah at once?

Abner found a ready reception to his suggestion. It met with instant approval from the elders of all the leading tribes in Israel. So with a special delegation of twenty men he set off for Hebron, there to inform David of Israel's desires.

It is a measure of David's character that he was prepared to meet Abner face to face so fearlessly. More than that, his generosity in preparing a magnificent banquet for his former foe and long-time rival does surprise us. As intimated earlier, David possessed a unique and amazing capacity to forgive those who wronged him. His magnanimous behavior was magnificent to behold.

Certainly it must have astonished Abner and those with him. The royal feast was not only an occasion to repair the old rifts between the two fighting generals from Bethlehem. Even more importantly it served to restore peace in this fractured nation so long torn by war and civil strife.

So impressed was Abner with David's open hand of friendship and goodwill extended to him that he vowed he would return home and recruit all of Israel for him.

He assured David that he would influence all of the tribes to give him their total allegiance so he could reign over the entire nation as a unified whole.

A peace pact was formed between the two men. With dignity and under his own personal protection, David then sent Abner away in safety and good will. What David had waited for so many years was suddenly within his grasp. What wonders Jehovah had worked out behind the scenes in response to the quiet faith of this patient monarch.

Beyond even that, David's generosity toward Abner demonstrated that indeed here was a man who was a true peacemaker, one who would choose to bring about reconciliation rather than hurtful discord. David was a man prepared to feed his foes to carry out the very explicit directions given to us by Christ for dealing with our enemies (read Matthew 5:9; 5:43–45 and Romans 12:18–21).

It is not surprising that in due course, despite some of David's dreadful mistakes, God would choose to refer to him as "a man after my own heart." That is to say one who, above all else, really did desire to do God's will.

It was no doubt a fortunate thing that Abner's visit to Hebron came at a time when Joab and his marauding men were away on a foray in enemy territory. Certainly, because Abner had killed his fleet-footed brother Asahel at Gibeon, David's general would never have allowed Abner even to enter Judean territory, let alone the king's city.

When Joab returned, with huge spoils of war, to find that Abner had been in Hebron and actually formed an alliance with David, he was beyond himself with rage. He had none of David's forgiving spirit. He knew nothing of pardon or peace. He was a furious and ferocious man bent on blood.

Without any hesitation he stormed into David's presence, his countenance black with anger, demanding why the king had done such a thing. Surely David was not so naive as to believe that Abner could be trusted? Did he not see that the enemy commander had simply come to reconnoiter the land? Did he not realize that Abner would only deceive and dupe him? And yet he let the adversary go in peace!

The angry charges tumbled out of Joab's mouth like chunks of molten lava erupting from a violent volcano. He was red hot with hate, utterly convulsed with a terrible white hot temper.

Immediately he left David in a rage. He dispatched a band of his men to bring Abner back to Hebron at once. There was a score to settle and he would do it without David even knowing anything about it.

Surprisingly enough, Abner returned at once. Perhaps David's banquet, his good will, his peace pact had lulled the cunning commander into believing all was well. Little did he dream that he was walking into a trap.

Joab waited for him at the city gate. Pretending that he had personal, private matters to discuss with his one-time boyhood friend from Bethlehem, Joab drew Abner aside from his associates.

Whispering something softly into Abner's ear, Joab drew his sword, a veritable flash of steel, and viciously plunged it into Abner's abdomen just below the fifth rib. It was the same brutal stroke with which his brother Asahel had been slain by Abner. The general fell to the ground dead. It was the ancient, cruel way of shedding blood for blood.

3

David's Response to the Deaths of Abner and Ishbosheth

As soon as the news of Abner's assassination was brought to David, the king was overcome with remorse. His spirit was torn by the grisly tragedy. He was mortified by the fact that the gallant general had fallen at the very gate of his own royal city ostensibly at a period of peace. He had come in confidence only to be cut down in one swift stroke like a ripened straw cut off by the reaper's scythe.

It was not that David was a stranger to bloodshed, murder and human brutality. He was not. Far from it! He himself had taken a grim toll of life. He had killed Goliath and severed the giant's head. He had deliberately, with the aid of other gallant young fighters, killed two hundred Philistines just to collect their foreskins as a dowry for Michal. He had led raid after raid into the enemy encampments of the Philistines and sleepy villages of the Amalekites, to wipe out every man, woman and child in cold blood.

No indeed, David's own hands had been stained dark with the blood of hundreds of victims. His sword had consumed countless lives. He was a man of war and violence. Why then should the sudden death of Abner cause him so much anguish? More especially when Abner had been his long time foe and deadly rival?

The answer is multifaceted. First and foremost, David felt his own reputation with all of Israel was at stake. Abner had come to Hebron with overtures of peace. He had been given David's protection in the name of peace. Now he had been murdered. Obviously most lay people would conclude the whole scene was a conspiracy on David's part to wipe out his opponent. Yet, in truth this time the king was absolutely innocent.

Second, David felt strongly that Joab's ruthless actions showed how much he scorned his monarch's might and disdained his sense of dignity. Or put another way, the assassination demonstrated that David was too weak to rule his kingdom well, that military men could do as they wished.

Third, there was no question David held Abner in high esteem for his military genius and capacity to consolidate Israel after Saul's death. He knew full well Abner was much more than a fierce warrior. He really had shown exceptional leadership at a difficult era in Israel's history.

To offset all of these adverse reflections on himself and his kingdom, David immediately disclaimed any responsibility for Abner's death. Instead he publicly announced that the consequences should fall upon Joab and his family.

It can be argued that David was too lenient in not executing more drastic judgment on Joab. A good case can be made for the death penalty to have been imposed upon the grisly general.

David decided not to take such extreme measures simply because it would no doubt have escalated into a clan war within his own family. More than that, it would have given Israel a further opportunity and reason to make war against Judah if the tribe were torn by internal strife.

Above all else what was needed now was bold, dramatic action that would unite the nation.

So as a compromise David denounced Joab and his family with a terrible curse. Its consequences would go on from generation to generation. In its train would come evil diseases, warfare, loss of life and grinding poverty.

The second startling step David took was to declare a national day of mourning for Abner. He would be given full military honors in his burial. And the entire armies of Judah would march in a full-dress parade to honor "the prince" fallen in Hebron.

To be buried in Hebron was to be granted the highest honor that could be bestowed by the nation on one of its heroes. Here Sarah had been entombed, so also Abraham, Isaac and Jacob. It was sacred ground reserved only for the most distinguished of the Hebrew people.

The full-dress parade would not be one of pomp and ceremony with gleaming armor and shining spears. Rather, under direct command from the king, Joab, Abishai and all his men would be garbed in drab sackcloth, with ashes on their heads, dust on their shoulders, in full mourning. Even David himself would walk in genuine grief behind the fallen general's bier.

It was to be an unforgettable day of lamentation for the entire nation. This epic event would draw together as one all the diverse and antagonistic elements in this obdurate people. It would refocus the attention of everyone upon the chief player in the drama—David himself.

As in the death of Saul, David raised his voice in an outpouring of grief and remorse for the one fallen. He bemoaned Abner's folly in forfeiting his life so easily to wicked men. He made his lament so poignant it touched and moved all of those present. It was not a staged play. It was the profound remorse of a fierce warrior who grieved for a fellow soldier cut down before his time.

When David declined to eat or drink all that day, but chose rather to fast as a supreme demonstration of his sorrow for the evil done in his kingdom, everyone knew his grief was genuine. It was a sure sign that he had played no part in the conspiracy to assassinate Abner. It convinced the whole nation that he was indeed a man of might who could be generous and magnanimous to others.

David's conduct in this incident was so far above reproach it pleased all the people—even his antagonists.

It was a master stroke of diplomacy and royal dignity that reassured Israel David well deserved their loyal allegiance. It was genuine good will overcoming evil intentions. It was wisdom and compassion quelling hostility. It was the spiritual life of the living God at work in David, dispelling the dark antagonisms of this dreadful day.

Once more the monarch's quiet confidence in the Lord's ability to lead him skillfully had been vindicated. As he was to say and assert repeatedly all through his long and troubled life, *"The LORD liveth, who has redeemed my soul out of all adversity."*

Publicly, openly, on this momentous occasion, David acknowledged that though he had been chosen of God and anointed to be king over his people, he really was too weak to deal with men as tough as Joab and Abishai. These ferocious and furious men of war would be a source of grief and aggravation to him the rest of his days. Remember, our Lord Jesus had in His close company tough young men like Judas, Peter, Thomas, James and John, the "sons of thunder." One might wonder why they were not just jettisoned. That is man's way. It is not God's divine design.

David realized, as did Christ, that the "hard people," the "tough characters," the "abrasive associates," whom God ordains to share our lives are there for two very specific purposes. The first is that these are the sharp tools, the cutting chisels, used by our Father to shape our characters into truly noble and beautiful proportions. So let us not try to escape from their rigorous action.

Second, difficult people constantly impinging upon us will drive us to seek our strength, patience and courage in Christ as nothing else in all the world. We will discover we cannot cope with hard people on our own. Like David, we acknowledge we are weak. But in our weakness our Father is given opportunity to show Himself strong and sure as He works and lives in us.

When the news of Abner's assassination reached the hapless Ishbosheth in Mahanaim, he was stricken with terror. The inept Israeli monarch sensed with profound intuition that his brief reign was coming to an end. Nor was he alone in this. Many of the common lay people in Israel who had not yet been made aware of Abner's moves to make peace with David felt sure their future was in great peril.

Among these was the poor family that provided food and shelter for Mephibosheth, a crippled lad who was the only remaining son of Jonathan, David's former dearest friend. The wee boy was only five years old when his heroic father, the finest prince in Israel, fell on Mt. Gilboa with his father, Saul, under the ferocious attack by the screaming Philistine archers.

In panic then, Mephibosheth's nurse had fled in fear for her life and that of her little charge. In her haste to escape she fell, and so did the child. He was so severely injured he was crippled for the rest of his life. Now a second time it seemed his life and future were in jeopardy as the dynasty of his grandfather, Saul, teetered on the edge of extinction. Little did he or his guardians dream of the amazing grace that would one day be extended to him by David.

In the midst of the mayhem and uncertainty now convulsing the nation, two tough young stalwarts from Gibeon decided the time was opportune to avenge their people on Saul's family. Their names were Rechab and Baanah. They lived among the people of Benjamin but their true roots were in Gibeon, the Canaanite tribe which had deceived Joshua in making a league with him. Later Joshua bound them into slavery to Israel to be hewers of wood and drawers of water for the Levites. But he also vowed solemnly that they should be preserved in perpetuity by Israel.

This sacred treaty Saul, in his misdirected folly, had broken. To try and win the general approval of Israel he had sent a contingent of his men to massacre the Gibeonites. It was a treacherous act (see 2 Samuel 21).

Now two of the survivors of that tragedy, Rechab and Baanah, decided to seek bloody retribution in settling the score by murdering Ishbosheth, Saul's remaining son. They crossed the Jordan valley and came boldly to the royal household at Mahanaim.

They had chosen an auspicious day for their grisly deed. The pathetic prince, so inept and impotent to rule his people, was in bed having an afternoon siesta. Only a servant woman winnowing grain seemed to be about the premises. Pretending that they had come to purchase wheat, they passed her readily and entered the royal chambers.

With utter ruthlessness they beheaded the king in his

bed, wrapped the bleeding head in a cloth and made their getaway. The whole dastardly deed was over in minutes, carried out with cruel cunning. That night the two conspirators traveled in glee across country, headed for Hebron, fifty miles away. In their hands they bore the terrible evidence of the king's demise.

The assassins were sure David would be more than delighted with the early death of Ishbosheth. With the single stroke of a sword not only had they avenged their own people of Saul's wrongs, but also they had brought a sudden end to his royal dynasty. Now David would no longer have a contender for the throne of Israel. The coast was clear for him to claim control over both Judah and Israel.

More than that, they were confident their action would also be seen as divine retribution on David's behalf for all the terrible tyranny Saul had exerted on him for so long. Nor did they hesitate to tell him so. But David did not agree.

His immediate response of horror, anger and utter revulsion at their criminal deed startled them. David replied as he so often did, "It is the Living God who has redeemed my soul out of all adversity." It was God who cared for him and spared him for His purposes. It was not for man to engineer and contrive cruel ways to achieve those ends.

With burning eyes and thundering tones, David reminded the two trembling murderers that their awful action exactly paralleled that of the arrogant Amalekite who had slain Saul on the battlefield. That foolish fellow, like them, had brought Saul's crown and bracelet to David as proof positive of his reprehensible deed. Perhaps naively he had assumed that he would be rewarded for bringing such grim news.

Instead, David ordered his immediate death. For he would countenance no one who raised a weapon of revenge against God's chosen and anointed royalty. Once again, David ordered that the two assassins standing before him be put to death immediately. They were wicked men who had crept into the king's house and murdered him in cold blood in his own bed. Once again the ancient law of blood for blood was enforced with formidable severity and terrifying speed.

Even more ghastly, their hands and feet, that had been so swift to shed innocent blood, were severed. The bleeding corpses were hung up in full view of the public at the pool in Hebron. It was a grim warning to all that they dare not take the law of revenge into their own hands.

As a final gesture of generosity and good will toward the ill-fated family of Saul, David commanded that Ishbosheth's royal head be buried in Abner's sepulcher in Hebron. Though the erstwhile king had been so weak, as a mark of his respect for God's anointed royal household, David insisted on this final salute to the rival monarch from Mahanaim.

4

David Consolidates His Rule over Israel at Jerusalem

David, king of Judah for seven years, was only thirty-seven years of age when all the nation of Israel came to him in Hebron to form a peace pact. The agony of the civil strife between his loyal followers and the dynasty of Saul was over. And in great wisdom the leaders of Israel declared, "We really are one. We are your bone and your flesh!"

More than that, however, they recognized it was the heroic exploits of David as a daring young warrior that had made it possible for his people to survive against their ancient foes—even when Saul was king. But beyond even this was their awareness that for fourteen long years, since Samuel anointed him to be king, it was Jehovah's intention for David to be their spiritual shepherd and their military monarch.

His hour of power had come.

All of Israel was bringing him their loyal allegiance.

Few monarchs would ever be so beloved and adored.

This was not only because of David's fighting prowess and administrative genius. It was also because he had been so closely identified with his people in every aspect of human suffering and dire extremity. He did not have the throne handed to him on a golden platter. He had come to it through exile, loneliness, despair, long delays, awful abuse, political tyranny and spiritual struggle.

Like the greater King, who is touched with the feelings of our infirmities, so David was bound into the bundle of life's sorrows which his people knew. In his poems, in his music, in his psalms he gave full play to all the full-orbed suffering of the family of man. And it is this, too, that has endeared him to every generation.

But now, in the prime of David's life, all Israel was consolidated under his command. This was no small thing. For they brought with them a huge army of 341,000 fighting men.

Seldom in human history had any cruel, civil conflict been resolved so swiftly or amicably. In large part it was the gracious generosity of David's spirit that made this possible.

So at Hebron, for the third time in his young life, David was anointed king, this time over all Israel. He took the honor very seriously. He saw it as a solemn charge from the Most High to govern God's chosen people with serious responsibility as a servant of the Lord.

With his long experience in battle, combined with a profound political expertise, David knew full well that some sort of dramatic action was needed now to weld all his warriors into a single formidable fighting unit. But beyond even that he saw the need to bind the whole nation together with a daring diplomatic move.

On the surface, from our perspective, his next move might seem a very simple step. But against the background of ancient tradition it was a tremendous challenge. He would move his royal palace to Jerusalem and there establish the spiritual sanctuary for the Most High.

At this point in history, Jerusalem stood stern, grim and unconquered as an enemy citadel in the heart of Israel. It was on the boundary between Judah on one side and the tribe of Benjamin on the other.

It was not the great sprawling city we see today. Instead it was a formidable fortress, utterly impregnable, that covered about eight acres of ground. The Jebusites who occupied it had never been brought into subjection by Israel. Even in the heyday of Joshua's mighty exploits in occupying Canaan, though he slew the king of Jerusalem, he could never occupy the citadel. Long years later he had to admit Judah could not take the city (see Joshua 15:63). Time rolled on and Jerusalem stood invincible. Nor could the tribe of Benjamin subdue the stronghold (Judges 1:21). For well over four hundred years it stood defiant in the heart of Israel.

Equally interesting is the fact that Melchisedech king of Salem (Jeru-Salem), "place of peace," was its first king. And on Mt. Moriah next to it, Abraham offered his son Isaac.

Not deterred by any of these long and terrifying traditions, David was determined to subdue the city and make it his own. He must have known someone in the citadel, for when he slew Goliath and severed his head, he took the grisly memento to Jerusalem. He also knew that the glorious Gihon spring had been tapped by an underground tunnel driven through solid rock. The water ran through this narrow channel (gutter) into a large pool beneath the fortress. From here there was a vertical, forty-foot shaft through which women could lower their leather buckets to draw up the sweet cool water.

Like General Wolfe (who stormed the heights of Abraham to capture Quebec city) David sensed that the only successful assault would have to be one made through this secret underground channel. To challenge his men for conquest, he offered the rank of full commanding officer to the first warrior to breach the defenses.

True to his tough character and unflinching ferocity Joab was the one who risked his very life to slip into the fortress, wading through water up to his waist. He was quickly followed by other doughty comrades and the citadel was stormed and captured from within—this in spite of all the taunts hurled at David from the defenders on its turreted walls.

Joab, despite having fallen from favor because of murdering Abner, was reinstated as David's commanding officer. The old ogre just would not go away. If need be, he would die for David and for the empire.

Being immediately on the border between Benjamin (Saul's tribe) and Judah (David's tribe), the location of Jerusalem was a strategic site politically. Like Washington, D.C., in the United States or Canberra A.C.T. in Australia, it was a brilliant diplomatic move. It would serve to unite all of Israel without partiality to any one tribe or segment of the nation. It was neutral ground.

In those distant days, it is doubtful indeed if David could ever dream of the dramatic as well as dreadful future this blood-stained city would have. Here in due time his son Solomon would erect the most beautiful temple ever built by man. Here there would be wars, ruin, raids and conquest, generation after generation. On this very site the Lord Jesus Christ would be condemned to death, to be crucified, to rise again, to ascend to glory. And, yes, to this site He will return again in power and great honor.

Today Jerusalem stands as the most significant city in all the world. Should it ever be proclaimed once more, as David did, to be the capital of Israel it will precipitate a global holocaust. A holy war, a Jahad, of international proportions will be triggered between Islam and the Western world which will be terrible beyond belief. Most westerners are exceedingly naive about this threat.

For David the conquest of Jerusalem was the first major military step he took to establish Israel as the dominant empire in the Middle East for fifty years. He was sending a signal to all the surrounding nations that the young lions of Judah and Israel were on the prowl. Soon nation after nation would fall prey to their attacks, coming under total domination.

Jerusalem from this time on bore several names. It was sometimes called *"The City of David"*; *"The royal city"*; *"Zion"*; *"Mt. Zion the city of our God"*; *"Jerusalem."* Quickly it came to be recognized as the center of power. Here David began to exert enormous influence far beyond the borders of his own nation. A truly mighty monarch had appeared on the stage of Israel's tragic history.

Even Hiram, tough king of Tyre on the Mediterranean coast, sensed he had to sue for peace. In good will he sent David skilled masons, carpenters and artisans to build him a magnificent palace of stone, cedar wood and gold.

Israel's hour of eclipse had passed.

This desolate people no longer huddled in the shadows.

David, under the strong hand of God, was bringing the nation out into the full blaze of its brightest days.

David had spiritual perception enough to realize that it was the Lord God who had exalted him to great power. He was also astute enough to see that this power was not for his own personal ends but to serve the best interests of the nation entrusted to him. Herein lay part of his heroic humility and also his potent spiritual influence.

46

David Consolidates His Rule over Israel at Jerusalem

He lived to please God and to serve His people.

In the midst of his ascent to ever-greater power and influence, David was plagued by a relentless propensity to polygamy. Of course, in the common culture of those times, a large part of a man's prestige was based upon his family. The more wives and children he could boast, the more esteem he held in the community. It has ever been thus in pagan communities among primitive people. But it most certainly was not God's original intention for the family of man.

For David the beautiful maidens of Jerusalem were irresistible. He took still more wives and concubines from among them. Eventually he was to have a considerable harem of some eighteen wives. And ultimately his desires in this direction would lead to the debacle with Bathsheba, which would cost him enormous pain and humiliation before the Most High.

As of old, Israel's ancient enemies, the Philistines, were not willing to relent in their attacks. Now that David had come to power in the nation one would assume that these people would hesitate to launch another offensive against him. Perhaps they had very short memories. For every time David had attacked them they had been soundly defeated.

It can be argued that because David had lived in exile among them, they had some sort of remote hope he might yet sue for peace. His friendship with Achish, king of Gath, was well known and possibly they thought his loyalty to him might induce David to come to some sort of terms with Israel's ancient foes. But it was not to be.

Rather, Israel's new monarch was a man determined to build a mighty empire. He had a clear and burning vision of what could be achieved for Israel with God's guidance. David was not content to let his people remain as a despised, second-rate power in the region. He would take up arms, go into battle, and extend Israel's empire far, far beyond its present borders. He had both the will and the military might to carve out a formidable state.

The Philistines' first assault came in the valley of Rephaim, commonly known as the "Valley of Giants." It lay southwest of Jerusalem, toward Bethlehem. David was wise and humble enough to seek the will of God as to whether he should attack the enemy at once. And if he did, he wished to have some sort of clear assurance that he would be victorious. The divine disclosure that came to him was to counterattack the Philistines at once. He was sure to conquer.

The result was a resounding triumph for his own troops. Still David declined to take credit for the victory. Instead, he declared boldly for all to hear: *"The LORD has broken forth upon my enemies as a flood of waters!"*

So thoroughly were the Philistines routed that they fled in terror abandoning the idols and effigies they had carried into battle. These the triumphant men of David gathered up into heaps and burned on the grim battlefield. Times had certainly taken a turn for the better since that grim day when the Philistines had cut off Saul's head and carried it around in triumph to be shown off before all their idols. Saul's armor, too, had been put on display in the temple of Ashteroth.

Obviously a deity greater than either Baal or Ashteroth was abroad in the land. The Lord Jehovah was with His people Israel in great power. He it was whom David desired to honor and serve with all his might.

Again, a second time, the pugnacious Philistines launched an attack in the same valley. For a second time, the determined David sought clear counsel from God as to how he should respond.

He was astute enough to know that experience alone from the first engagement was not sufficient to assure him success. The clear instruction given to him was that this time he should encircle the Philistines from behind. And when there was the unmistakable sound, as of a wind blowing the trembling leaves in the tops of the trees (mulberry, poplar, balsam), then David should attack, for the Lord God was going into action before him.

Once more the engagement was a tremendous triumph for David. In fact, the enemy was routed all the way along the coast from Geba to the famous Gaza strip.

David had been given clear guidance from God. He carried out God's command without debate. The result was a resounding victory.

That is a very basic principle for success in our daily walk with God. We cannot, we dare not rely on past experience to guide us in our conflicts with the relentless enemy of our souls. Instead, in each encounter we need to seek clear instructions from Christ. He will direct us implicitly what to do. Our part then is to quietly, quickly, comply with His commands and do what He asks. This is the formula for overcoming the enemy. David knew it!

5

David Brings the Ark to Jerusalem

To his great credit, David had now achieved three significant goals. In the realm of civic affairs, he had established himself as a splendid statesman of the first rank in uniting his people despite their deep divisions. Second, he had shown remarkable intuition and political astuteness in establishing the nation's new capital in the city of Jerusalem, on neutral ground, claimed from the enemy. Third, he had again demonstrated his remarkable military leadership in routing the Philistines.

Such strategic and dramatic demonstrations of power, skill and generalship would have more than satisfied most men at his age (about forty years). But David was no ordinary man in such matters. He was a monarch who saw himself as the servant of an even greater Majesty than his own. He saw his role clearly of being God's spiritual under-shepherd to Israel.

He recognized the terrible truth that for nearly seventy years Israel had seriously neglected her spiritual life as a people. The Ark of the Lord had been almost forgotten. The priesthood had been slaughtered by Saul. The Levites no longer had the great honor of ministering to the Most High as they should. And the people were, like so many of our so-called Christian countries of the twentieth century, becoming more and more pagan.

David was determined to change all this. He was sure that once again, as in the days of Joshua, he could provide the powerful, personal leadership that would challenge Israel to seek God and serve Him in humble obedience. To initiate this dramatic change in direction he decided the Ark of the Lord should be brought up to Jerusalem and put in a place of prominence in the capital city.

This was not just a clever gimmick to titillate the spiritual aspirations of Israel. It was a powerful move that would restore the very presence of the Most High in an imposing and preeminent position in the life of the people. All the focus and attention of the common people would again be centered on the person of Jehovah God.

From the tremendous days during which God had met with Moses on the burning, smoking summit of Sinai, there to give him the laws of life for His chosen people, the Ark carried enormous import. It denoted the very presence of God; it bore the covenant promises of power vested in Him. It was the place of pardon and peace where the Almighty met with men at the sacred mercy-seat. It bore the law of God.

Once again David was determined that the Ark be elevated to its proper place of prominence in Israel. As the Shepherd King, responsible to God for the spiritual health and well-being of his stubborn and obdurate nation, this simply had to be the first priority.

Because it was so long since the Ark had been moved, no doubt David and his contemporaries had forgotten all the very explicit instructions regarding its transportation. These are stated clearly in the book of Numbers

(4:5–20 and 7:1–9). Briefly, they were that it should never be carried in a cart or drawn by animals, but always borne high in full view of the people on the broad, strong shoulders of the clan of Kohath, a sacred Levite family. Not one of them should dare touch the sacred chest, much less even open it to examine the sacred contents.

In the tragic times of the aged prophet Eli, the Ark had fallen into the hands of the Philistines. Wherever it was taken terrible consequences followed. Wondering what to do, the Philistines consulted their occult leaders who directed that a cart be built in which it was to be hauled back to Israel. The cows used to do this, even though with calves at heel, returned the sacred chest to everyone's surprise.

Perhaps looking back to that remarkable episode, David and his advisers decided to do the same thing, forgetting it was diametrically disobedient to God's directions. The results were to be drastic for David. Though he had the best of intentions and loftiest motives, he was doing the wrong thing in the wrong way.

The Ark was picked up and placed in the cart built for it. It was thought that Ahio and Uzzah, the two sons of Abinadab, on whose property the Ark had stood in disuse for so long, were familiar with it. Therefore, they would be well able to drive the team hauling it.

As they got under way a huge and joyous crowd of people from all over Israel accompanied the Ark. David had assembled some 30,000 representatives from all over the nation to participate in this spiritual celebration. There was a massed choir of chanting voices plus a huge orchestra of musicians playing songs of praise on every sort of wind or stringed instruments.

Suddenly amid all the exultation and jubilation, such as Israel had not seen in fifty years, the cart jolted over some rough ground. It looked for an instant as if the Ark would tip over, it was shaken so badly. In his hasty impulse Uzzah grabbed the sacred chest to keep it from crashing to the ground. It was a fatal move! He fell dead behind the cart. He had, in his haste, well intentioned as it was, ignored the clear and explicit edict given never to touch the Ark.

The sudden, drastic event stilled all the people. David was distraught and greatly grieved. It was a sobering moment for everyone. In very truth, the Most High was among His people. Now they were acutely aware He must be approached with reverence, awe and the enormous respect His Majesty deserved. For David it was a solemn reminder of his own fallible humanity.

The celebration was cut short in midsession. With deep soul-searching David wondered if indeed he was worthy to have the Ark even brought into Jerusalem. Perhaps it should be set up in another site? Maybe he had been too presumptuous in planning to share the royal city with the Most High God?

In contrition of spirit David ordered the Ark moved to the home of a Levite named Obed-Edom. It was a wise decision. For Obed-Edom was a Gittite, one of the descendants of the Korahites or Kohathites who had been ordained of God so long ago to bear the Ark. In his home the sacred chest stood for three long months. And there it brought unusual blessing and benefits to Obed-Edom and his family. It was the right thing being done in the right way in accordance with the explicit wishes of the Lord.

There is imbedded in this incident a lesson of enormous consequence to the church of our day. Simply stated in layman's language it is this: "All the planning; all the programs; all the praise and dramatic displays of man's devising come to nothing if they are not in clear compliance with our Father's will and instructions to us."

In His integrity, justice and honor, God will not countenance disobedience or human disregard for His laws. Even though we may have the best of intentions, if they contravene His commands the end result can be destruction.

Just as David and his associates chose a pagan, worldly way to try to do God's work, so in many cases the contemporary church tries to use the world's techniques and technology to achieve spiritual results. Again and again the results are ruin. We need desperately to search our souls and examine our spirits to be sure we do God's work, in His way, according to His will.

David, with his spirit so attuned to the Spirit of God, was acutely aware of the great wrong committed. He knew without doubt that repentance and remorse were required to restore his personal relationship to Jehovah in this breach between them. He summoned the priests, and Levites as well, and ordered them to make the proper preparations necessary to move the Ark in dignity, awe and respect, as ordained by the living God.

This meant that they would have to take elaborate steps to cleanse and sanctify themselves for the occasion. They would have to select only Levites from the family of Kohath to pick up and actually bear the Ark high on their shoulders for all the people to see. Last, they would have to prepare pure, spotless oxen and rams, seven of each, to offer as sacrifices of propitiation and peace to insure that the move was wholly in accord with the wishes and will of the Most High. More maybe even than that, the sacrifice was to atone for the wrong done in using a pagan method of bringing the Ark into Jerusalem.

Perhaps we may feel all of this was excessive. But let

it not be forgotten the great respect demanded by God for His own presence and His own Word. These were both combined in the Ark. It was the Ark which was ordained to lead and direct God's people. It was the Ark which held absolute preeminence in the Holy of Holies. It was the Ark which David was now restoring to a place of prominence in Israel in order to *bring God and His people together again.*

The king also ordered that elaborate arrangements be made again by the Levites to assemble and train whole choirs of vocalists for the occasion. They were to be accompanied by magnificent groups of musical instruments of every sort to give worthy honor and praise to God.

Most wonderful, God Himself aided them in all of this!

Finally the great day came for the celebration. No sooner was the sacred chest lifted high on the shoulders of its bearers, and six steps taken, the appropriate sacrifices were offered for sins and atonement with God. The slaying of seven oxen and seven rams marked the absolution of all who participated in the celebration.

For David, it was much more than a religious rite. It was the release from his remorse; the restoration of his joy in the Lord after profound repentance; the liberation of his whole person from fear of having offended the Almighty.

In jubilation and pure adoration he began to leap and bound into the air with exhilaration. His poetic soul and artistic nature had to find full expression of gratitude in acknowledging that God, very God, deigned once more to come and dwell among His people.

Lest he should in any way detract the people's attention from the Ark by adorning himself in gorgeous royal robes, David attired himself only in a plain white robe covering a simple servant's tunic beneath. He was God's servant.

He insisted he be seen by all his people that way. It made a profound impact on everyone in the procession as it approached the elaborate tabernacle prepared by David to house the Ark.

A rising crescendo of singing, shouting, hand-clapping, music, blowing of bugles and sound of trumpets accompanied the parade into the city. Israel had not witnessed such a spectacle for fifty years, since the great day on which their first king, Saul, was crowned. Now, even greater glory and honor were being lavished upon His Majesty, the Most High God. Today David, his people, and the city of Jerusalem were "receiving" heaven's royalty.

Put in another way it could well be said that Israel, which had rejected God and chosen Saul as their king, had made an about-face and were reinstating the living God in His appropriate place of regal power and authority over them.

Only a monarch as humble in heart and lowly in spirit as David could ever have achieved such a spiritual triumph. On this memorable occasion God took great delight in coming to dwell among His chosen people. They had honored Him. He in turn would honor and bless them in magnificent ways beyond their fondest dreams.

Once the Ark had been set in its prepared place of preeminence in the tabernacle, David ordered more momentous sacrifices and peace offerings to be made. This was to insure that every step taken had been in accordance with God's will. It was to confirm that complete propitiation had been made for every person who had assembled in the celebration. They came from every hamlet, village and town of the sprawling nation.

It was a day of national blessing. It was an hour of

glory and honor and adulation for Jehovah God. In dramatic ecstasy and poetic fervor David composed the magnificent psalm recorded for us in 1 Chronicles 16:7–36. Few are the psalms anywhere that match this one for the honor, majesty, might, glory and power poured out upon the Person of God. Oh, what exaltation of the Most High!

Aloud before all his people he dedicated this tribute to the living God. They must have been moved to utter exuberance by his praise and adoration. He was their spiritual leader, leading them to reverence their God, leading them to worship the Lord in the beauty of holiness.

His face radiant and aglow, shining with the joy of God's Spirit, David then raised his sunburned arms aloft and turned to bless his people. His eyes were tender, caring, compassionate toward these sheep entrusted to his shepherd care.

"The LORD bless thee, and keep thee:
The LORD make his face shine upon thee,
and be gracious unto thee:
The LORD lift up his countenance
upon thee, and give thee peace" (*Numbers 6:24–26*).

Each one was then given a loaf of bread, a flagon of wine and a delicious piece of meat. It would be hearty fare to sustain them on their trek home. What happy feet would tread the dusty trails across every inch of Israel. All was well!

Or, so it seemed, until David returned to his own royal palace. There he came with jubilant spirit and overflowing heart to bestow a special benediction of blessing on his own household. What he had done for the whole nation he wished to do in particular for his own family.

He was met at the door by a glowering, angry, fuming wife. Michal, Saul's daughter, a princess in Israel, with the right to be queen of the realm for she was David's first wife, was in a towering rage. From the outset of the day's celebration she had refused to have any part in it. She had, instead, simply sulked in her upstairs room. She should have been singing, dancing, playing a tambourine, leading the ladies in joyous songs.

But no! She would have no part of it. She chose to sit alone, aloof, proud, haughty, arrogant, looking down with utter disdain upon David who danced with such joy before His God. She would never deign to so humble herself. She would never display herself in such a demeaning and menial manner. What a fool David was! What a disgrace to the kingdom! What a source of gossip for the lips of young ladies!

David was not deterred by her vicious diatribe. He simply replied quietly, "It was God who chose me to succeed your father Saul. It is He who has exalted me to rule over His people. I will play my part before Him. I will humble myself in His presence. And in due time He in turn will honor me before all His people, even these girls."

Nothing more was said. Michal not only despised David, she did not share his love for God. She was jealous of his devotion in doing God's will. Her bitterness, her animosity only drove David to seek his consolation the more deeply in God. The result was he composed Psalms 15, 22, 24, 29, 30, 132 and 141 at this magnificent time of his reign.

As for this despicable woman, her destiny was to be

58

barren and childless for all her days. She was a fruitless wife, a grief to herself and to God.

What she had failed to realize is that it is a most dangerous attitude to despise another. For God, very God, by His Spirit resides in other lives just as He does in ours. And in despising them we may well risk despising Christ.

6

David Is Denied the Honor to Erect God's Temple

The jubilant installation of the Ark in Jerusalem was a mountain peak of special spiritual significance to David. It stood like a shining snowfield high above the clouds of war and dark valleys of desperation which had filled so much of his tempestuous and stormy life.

Very much as it did with Peter, James and John, with our Lord on the Mount of Transfiguration, the brightness and effulgence of the hour was so rapturous it ignited a profound desire in David to perpetuate the glory by erecting a temple on the spot. Somehow it seemed only a noble sanctuary for the residence of the Most High could sustain the spiritual splendor in that spot.

The concept of building a beautiful temple may or may not have originated with David. My view is that the idea really began with Samuel, the great prophet of God and the last of the judges. From his days a portion of all the spoils of war were set aside in a special treasury fund for the use of the tabernacle and with the thought in mind that as an established nation Israel should consider the construction of a permanent, proper "House of the Lord" (see 1 Chronicles 26:20–28).

All through Saul's reign, under the direction of Abner, then in David's rule, under Joab, huge sums of money as well as precious metals and stones were put into the tabernacle treasury toward this end. Now with David in power, the time seemed appropriate to him for such a building to be erected—the more so when he himself already occupied a royal mansion of grand design and impressive proportions.

When the king shared his sentiments with Nathan the prophet he was met with immediate encouragement. "By all means, David, do whatever you will. God is with you. A splendid idea!" The temple had long been a national dream.

Although the building of a magnificent sanctuary was a noble aspiration, a generous gesture on David's part, this was not the man nor the era which God Himself had chosen for its construction. God made this abundantly clear to Nathan that very same night. The prophet had been too hasty, too human, in urging the king to proceed with the project.

A true prophet is one who receives a clear command from the living God and is bold enough, even at great risk to himself, to deliver that word directly to those who should receive it. In a dramatic about-face, the trusty Nathan had to return the next day and advise the monarch that his exuberant advice the day before had been dead wrong. Not easy to do! Again and again Nathan was the man of God who would confront David in his hours of crisis, bringing him to face formidable truth with drastic consequences.

Now Nathan had to break the hard news to David that

he would be denied the honor, the joy and the deep satisfaction of erecting a gorgeous temple for his God. This was a special responsibility that would be entrusted to his son (Solomon)—a prince of peace who would emerge from David's loins.

With great care and genuine compassion the Lord had given Nathan a lengthy message. He recognized that David's intentions were noble and upright. He understood that his heart (his will) and all of its motives were pure and proper. Building the temple was not to exalt himself, but to honor the Most High.

The best will in the world is not good enough unless that will also works in accord with the will of God. It must be in harmony with the way He chooses and the time He selects and the place He appoints. This would be the tough lesson David had to learn from Nathan that day. And most of us as God's people are slow indeed to learn it until the end of our days. The reason we have trouble with it lies in our innate human pride.

God made this very clear to the prophet and to David. He stated categorically in so many words, "I didn't ask you to build me a temple. I didn't tell you I needed a structure of stone and cedar to dwell in. I have been perfectly content to occupy a tent made of skins; to dwell in a movable tabernacle among my people wherever they went since leaving Egypt.

"To build a temple is your idea not Mine. Still all the honor, all the power, all the fame that came to Israel and to David, really came from *Me*, Jehovah God. I AM, the One who has made it possible for this people to become an established nation: I AM, the One who has chosen David and raised him to great prominence among the rulers of the earth: I AM, the One who subdues your enemies all around, is also the One who will indeed 'make you a house.' "

Those last few words were pregnant with spiritual truth far transcending anything David may have dreamed possible at that time. For in truth, as will be seen toward the end of this book, it was God Himself who would reveal and transmit to David every architectural detail, measurement and dimension of the temple to be erected. It would be by implicit divine revelation that the blueprints and plans for all of the temple and its courts would be entrusted to David. The whole process and procedure were identical to those of the divine designs entrusted to Moses on Mt. Sinai for the construction of the tabernacle, the Ark and all its utensils.

All of this data, all of these details, all of these explicit plans David would pass on to his son Solomon. And with them David would also provide all the gold, silver, bronze, iron, stones and other materials for its erection.

The total treasury assembled by David for the project would eventually be calculated in astronomical sums exceeding billions of dollars. Oh, the days ahead would be charged with incredible excitement as the king saw the Lord's largesse grow and multiply beyond belief. He would derive as much joy in preparing for the temple in abundance as he would have had in building it now. Probably much more, because anything erected now would have been much, much less splendid than what could be constructed at the conclusion of his illustrious life.

The later glory would be a much greater splendor!

But beyond all of this house of wood and stone, the Eternal assured David through Nathan that it was also his family household, his dynasty, that would be built and established forever by the Lord. Saul's regency had been rejected because of disobedience to God's will. David's descendants would be assured of continuity, not because of any spotless behavior, but simply because God had found in David a man who, despite his failings, was determined at any cost to do God's will.

No matter how far from the paths of righteousness some of David's heirs might stray, still, because of His own covenant with this man this day, David's name would be held in honor. His family would provide the royal lineage through which the Greater David, Jesus Christ, the Messiah, foretold by the prophets, would come (see Matthew 1:1 & Luke 1:32).

The last sense in which God's intention for David was to "make you a house," was just that—exactly as it is for each of us who know and love Him. Our Father's fondest desire is that we become His temple, His house, His building in which He delights to reside. Above everything else God would demonstrate through David's life that He could do just this. Despite David's faults, despite his failures, despite his fears, God could come into that life and by His presence and power make it a fit habitation for the Most High.

The solemn commitment, the binding covenant made by God to David on this momentous day equaled that given to Abraham more than 760 years before. It would reach down through the long centuries yet to come until the day dawned when God Himself in human guise would enter the lineage of this monarch to be born as a tender child in a sheepcote outside of Bethlehem.

David was great enough in mind, sensitive enough in spirit not to be rebuffed by Nathan's message of denial. Unlike most men in his position of power he did not feel put down by God's refusal to let him build his beloved temple. He knew full well, as afterward he would confess to both Solomon and all of Israel, that his war-torn career shaped by hands so stained with shedding human blood were not suited to be chosen to erect a sanctuary for the glory and honor of the Most High.

Without rancor, argument or protest, this gracious, humble ruler went quietly to the skin-covered tabernacle and there offered up one of the most moving prayers recorded in Scripture. It was that rare prayer of total acceptance and self-relinquishment seldom uttered by the sons of men.

Sitting softly, subdued, utterly sincere before the Sovereign of all the earth, David acknowledged his own unworthiness and that of his family. He saw with undimmed clarity what an enormous honor it was for him to be chosen to rule God's chosen people.

"Who am I, Oh, LORD God?"—This was the fervent, passionate cry of any contrite soul seeking for the ultimate reality of knowing itself, and knowing the living God. Yet within that profound question David discovered the answer that stilled his spirit and assured his soul, *"He was God's chosen Child—beloved of the Father."*

This is the ultimate answer each of us, who long to know and love God, must find. It is not who I am that matters half as much as *whose* I am. To discover that God has chosen us in love before the foundation of the world to become His adopted sons and daughters is to have our souls set free into a dimension of amazing assurance. For David this was a liberating truth.

He goes on to declare, not with fear or apprehension, but in ecstatic delight, *"Oh, LORD God, Thou knowest Thy servant!"* He was no stranger to the Omnipotent One. He was no newcomer to the gracious presence of the Most High. He stood, stripped, exposed yet unashamed in full view of God who knew him through and through.

In later life David was to compose an entire psalm devoted to this theme. Psalm 139 stands in all of human literature as one of the most searching statements ever penned about the all-knowing omniscience of our God. In it, David, writing under the unction of the Spirit of God, reveals how God, and only God, fully understands and knows each of us.

On this great day David saw with clear spiritual perception that even though the Almighty knew every intimate detail of his life, He still loved him, still chose him, for special service. Such awareness, such knowledge overwhelmed the king. Despite David's weakness, despite his human fallibility, despite his days of despair and darkness, despite his lapses, God in His own great grace and sovereign love chose him to be His servant in fulfilling His purposes for His people.

Such knowledge was what humbled him in the hand of the Most High. Little wonder David loved Him so much.

More than all of this; more than what God had done for him as a mere man; more than what He would do for him as a monarch in a mighty empire was what the Lord God intended to do with David's people, Israel.

This was no ordinary nation. It was a special chosen race, through whom it was destined *"the Deliverer"* would come to save all men from their sins. God, very God, had redeemed them for Himself. He would pay the supreme price of His own substitutionary death for their deliverance. This He had ordained from before the foundation of the earth. This He would do, using the dynasty of this devoted monarch to achieve His ultimate ends.

David Is Denied the Honor to Erect God's Temple

Not only could David foresee the future of God's plans for His people, but also he had sufficient spiritual sensitivity to recognize what a signal honor it was for him, as an individual, to play a large part in those plans. True, God was building the house and lineage through which salvation would come both to Israel and David's successors, but it would also be the means through which light would come to the entire world—a light to lighten the Gentiles as well.

Finally, triumphantly, the house built by God would not only be ten billion individual souls in whom His gracious Spirit chose to reside, each as the temple of God, but also He was building the house of God in the form of the family and household of God the Father. Each of us has been given the glorious opportunity to enter and enjoy that house, if we so choose.

David understood this broad and magnificent concept. In earnest petition he held God to His covenant. He stood upon the unequivocal statements of God Himself that these were His promises and therefore were self-binding. He was utterly confident that the Most High would bless His own purposes for all men; that He would pour out His special benefits on Israel; that He would be an eternal benediction to David as the shepherd of His sheep. In this knowledge he was content and at peace!

7

David's Conquests and His Care for Mephibosheth

This is an appropriate place to pause briefly in the narrative of David's life to reiterate what was pointed out in *David I.* Namely, that my interest in this work as an author is primarily with David's personal response to God's overtures, rather than with the details of his military conquests from an historical point of view.

The record given to us in Scripture bears out the validity of such an approach. Entire chapters of God's Word are devoted to a single spiritual struggle David had within his soul and spirit. On the other hand, in other places the sweeping subjection of entire enemy states is covered in a few brief verses.

From God's perspective the establishment of His house, the extension of His kingdom in a single soul is of greater consequence than the conquest of human empires. The man or woman whose life becomes a dynamic part of the very kingdom of the living God endures forever. Earthly empires rise and fall, fading into oblivion.

Understanding this concept helps us recognize clearly that the original Author of the biblical record was indeed the very Spirit of God Himself. So in following His leading, less importance is given to military matters than many might wish to find in a book of this kind.

There is, of course, no question but that David was a ferocious fighting man who could be ruthless in battle. He had a remarkable capacity for leadership to which his warriors responded valiantly even against formidable odds. He was a fearless national hero. Men risked their lives for him gladly. His name became a byword throughout the empires of the east. More often than not, he and his forces were triumphant. He came home the victor with huge quantities of spoils and booty from battle after battle.

Not only was he taking vast areas of new territory for his growing empire, he was adding huge wealth to its treasury. By the time he had conquered and subdued all the nations around Israel, his empire extended from the banks of the Euphrates River in the north to the river of Egypt—(not the Nile)—in the south. It stretched from the Trans-Jordan region of Moab and Ammon on the east to the Mediterranean coast on the west (see map on next page).

One of David's first conquests was Methegammah. This was the stronghold of Gath in Philistine territory—the very city where twenty years before he had fled as an exile from Saul's anger. He had scrabbled on its gate, feigning madness to gain entrance. Now the citadel fell to his forces like a toppled domino, establishing his power over Israel's ancient foe.

Next David's forces swooped down into the formidable broken country and desert ranges of Moab. This people had always opposed Israel. Even though David's maternal grandmother, Ruth, had come from Moab, no love was lost between the two warring nations. In his fear for their

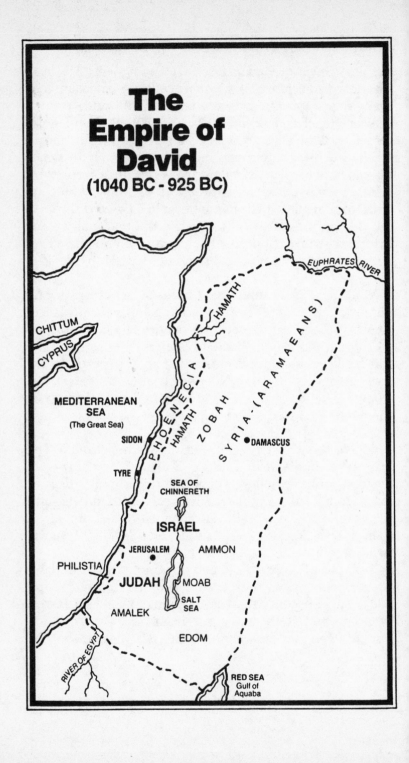

The Empire of David
(1040 BC - 925 BC)

safety, David had sent his own parents to Moab hoping they would find refuge there from Saul's madness. But it was not to be. For ancient tradition has it that they were treacherously murdered there.

So now in fierce retribution two thirds of the entire population were wiped out in the triumph of war, the remaining third brought into total subjection. From then on they would be a vassal state within David's empire that would pay him enormous annual tribute.

The next region to come under attack from Israel was called Zobah. It extended from the nation's northern borders near the headwaters of the Jordan all the way to the tributaries of the Euphrates. Its ruler was Hadadezer, who had both foot soldiers and cavalry units with chariots.

In a bitter battle David took 20,000 of his footmen from the foreign king as well as a thousand chariots. This was no mean accomplishment, since Israel had no cavalry. From the time of the great Exodus from Egypt in which Egypt's horses and chariots pursued Israel, the Hebrews had been forbidden to muster chariots and horses. It will be recalled that Joshua in conquering Canaan had always given explicit orders that the enemy horses be destroyed and their chariots burned with fire.

The same was now done by David, except for one hundred chariots. The reason was that God always knew Israel would be tempted to return to Egypt to find the finest horses and chariots. He did not want Israel to depend on cavalry for conquest, but on Himself. In fact, David states this emphatically in Psalm 20:7: *"Some trust in chariots and some in horses: but we will remember the name of the LORD our God."*

Not until the days of Solomon did Israel turn back to Egypt to purchase large numbers of horses and chariots.

This was but part of the great evil which would lead to a collapse of empire.

In his conquest of Zobah, David amassed huge quantities of gold from the shields of the warriors. Then he collected from other smaller cities mountains of brassware for which these people were famous. All of this booty was then transported to Jerusalem, much of it to be set aside for the treasury of the tabernacle (the temple fund).

The Syrians, ancient allies, hearing of Zobah's defeat came to their aid. The results were disastrous for the desert raiders. In swift and violent action David's rampaging young lions slew 22,000 of them in battle. It was a brutal and bloody victory.

As he did with Moab and Zobah David set up strong Israeli garrisons in the city of Damascus and all across the desert wastes. These saw to it that regular tribute was paid in "gifts of silver, gold, brass."

The next region to come under David's influence was that of Hamath. This was the country lying between the ranges of Lebanon and Anti-Lebanon. Its king, Toi, sent his royal son Joram to sue for peace with David, bringing with him magnificent princely gifts of gold, silver and brass.

In genuine gratitude to God for all His benefits, David chose to dedicate most of these rare and beautiful treasures to the Lord. There is no question some of the wealth coming from his wars of conquest was kept for his own royal estate. Yet by far the larger portion was given gladly to God's service.

Such generosity toward the Most High stands as a signal monument to the memory of this great man of God. To the end of his days David did not allow wealth to corrupt his character. He recognized clearly that all possessions and the ability to amass wealth were granted to him by the generosity of God. So he in turn was happy and eager to return most of it to the Giver.

God honored him for this gracious attitude. No matter where his now famous armed forces moved in great might they met with success. Even Edom far to the south in the Negev desert was brought into total subjection to Jerusalem. Wherever David extended His empire God was there to preserve and establish His power.

This is not surprising—first of all, because this vast region had been promised by God to Abraham, to Moses, to Joshua. And David was simply carrying out the divine decree declared so long before to his forebears (see Genesis 15:18).

More than being just a military genius David also ruled Israel as a superb statesman. He set up highly respected leaders in the nation to administer justice, to fulfill all the spiritual responsibilities of the priesthood, to keep careful records of civil affairs and to care for the education and welfare of his people.

Unlike many national leaders who either tend to be politicians or despots, David was able to rule in a bold, nonpartisan manner that won him the loyal allegiance of all Israel. This in itself was a splendid achievement. He refused to pander to any special interest groups. So in truth it could be said of him, *"David executed judgment and justice unto all his people. And the LORD preserved David whither soever he went."*

It is no wonder Israel flourished under his monarchy. Few indeed are statesmen ever found of his caliber.

Though David was now approaching the pinnacle of his power in the affairs of the empire, he was not so engrossed with grand designs that he forgot his former friends. Proof of this lay in the deeply touching account given to us by God's Spirit of this man's generosity to Jonathan's son, Mephibosheth.

Roughly twenty tempestuous years had elapsed since those heady days when David had been Israel's young hero, the slayer of Goliath, the favorite in Saul's court. It was then that unbreakable bonds of loyalty were built between the two gallant young warriors. In fervent friendship David vowed to Jonathan that no matter how forbidding the future might be, he would care for and preserve his friend's posterity—either in life or in death.

It was destined to be in death. Jonathan fell in battle before the Philistines on Mt. Gilboa. When the dreadful news came, the nurse entrusted with the little son Mephibosheth, fled in terror, dropping the baby in her panic. He was crippled in both legs and simply seemed to drop out of public view. Even Michal, David's wife, and the baby's aunt, seemed to have no idea where he was. Being the sort of person she was, perhaps she didn't even care. At least she never told David.

David was not to be deterred by this indifference. He ordered that a nationwide search be made to see if in fact any member of Jonathan's family still survived. He was determined at any cost to carry out his own personal commitments to his friend.

Eventually one of Saul's royal retainers, a man by the name of Ziba, was found. He knew all about Mephibosheth. Like so many people appointed to special service in royal households Ziba was a cunning opportunist. He was a "survivor," one of those crafty individuals who amid the upheavals and mayhem of the times managed to do very nicely for himself. All the while he pretended to care for the property entrusted to him.

David summoned Ziba to give an account of Jonathan's son. To the king's dismay and chagrin he learned that

Mephibosheth was subsisting in utter poverty. And, to make matters worse, he lived in a destitute spot called Lodebar which means—*"Nothing"!*

Ziba himself, on the other hand, had managed to acquire quite an estate for himself out of the royal holdings left by Saul. He had a substantial harem, with fifteen sons, to say nothing of his large retinue of twenty servants. Yes, he was very comfortable indeed.

David ordered him to bring Mephibosheth to Jerusalem at once. The poor cripple would have to be carried at least fifty miles across country to the royal palace. He came in abject terror, sure he would be charged for the awful cruelty perpetrated by his grandfather, Saul, against David. Strange and impossible as it sounds, no one must ever have told him about the beautiful friendship that flourished between his father, Jonathan, and David. It has to be one of the best kept secrets in human society for all time!

David immediately put the young man at ease. "Fear not," he said. "For your father's sake I will restore to you all the property that belonged to Saul, all the fields, all the crops, all the flocks and herds. But most important you will dine at my royal table as though you were one of my own sons, a veritable prince in Israel."

David could not have shown Mephibosheth any greater kindness. He could not have bestowed on the destitute youth any greater honor. He could not have enriched his life to any greater degree, nor impressed Israel more.

In a swift and cunning move that was more than a match for the crafty Ziba, David then ordered him, his sons and his servants to be fully responsible to Mephibosheth. He would have to work his land, tend his fields, care for his livestock and see to it that the entire estate was managed efficiently for his new master.

75

It probably took Ziba's hot breath clean away. It was such a sudden and dramatic turn in events he could do nothing but accede to David's demands. At least this time the wily old scoundrel had been out-foxed. Most important, justice had been done. Kindness had its day. And David's love had raised a man to honor.

Mephibosheth was overwhelmed. He had seen himself as nothing, of no account, as only a dead dog! Now suddenly he had been given dignity, respect and recognition in the royal household. He had literally been adopted into David's family as a royal son.

This is precisely the picture of the even greater generosity of our Most High King. It is He who comes to seek us, to find us, to pick us up in our poverty and despair. It is He who in loving kindness and tender mercy extends to us His love. He invites us to share the bounties of His household. He bestows on us the honor to be His sons and daughters!

Little marvel He declares that love lasts forever, that it endures beyond any earthly empire, that it is the greatest good in all the world!

8

The Conquest of Ammon

The nation of Ammon was, for the greater part of its history, a nomadic desert race, descended from the younger son of Lot. They were often opposed to Israel and had made nefarious leagues with the other desert tribes to try and prevent Israel from occupying all of the territory promised to it by the Most High.

During Saul's era of tyranny their king had been Nahash. He was a cruel and formidable foe who threatened to attack Jabesh-gilead and enslave them as a people. In their peril they appealed to young King Saul for help. In the most heroic action of his entire life, Saul mustered all the men of Israel by sending butchered slabs of beef throughout the entire nation. It was a grim warning that the same fate would befall any man who did not rally to his call.

Within twenty-four hours Saul had assembled a huge force. These he led across the Jordan and by a night march came against Ammon in a surprise attack that routed the enemy with great victory. All of Israel was jubilant and in their triumphant celebration crowned Saul a second time to commemorate the occasion. The people of Jabesh-gilead never did forget Saul's great deliverance from Ammon. So when the tragic king was killed in combat by the Philistines, it was their young men who were brave enough to retrieve the corpses of Saul and his three sons from the enemy to give them proper burial.

During the subsequent years the fierce nomadic King Nahash, archenemy of Saul, must have come to some sort of terms with David. Or it may even have been that during David's exile, he was given refuge or supplies to escape Saul's attacks. We simply are not told. But Nahash had shown David special kindness.

Now, suddenly, in a strange twist of events David felt constrained to send a delegation of his officials to Hanun, son of Nahash, as a sign of respect, honor and condolence for his father's death. Such things do happen in the complicated world of diplomacy. Nor was it unlike David for he was always quick to repay the loyalty and friendship shown to him by others.

Unfortunately his intentions, though sincere, were not interpreted as such by Hanun's counselors. They were suspicious, just as Joab had been when Abner came to see David, that there were ulterior motives behind the mission. They suspected it was a clever ruse to spy out the city and so plan an attack on Ammon.

The question put to Hanun was blunt: *"Do you really believe David wishes to honor your father? Rather, he has sent these men as spies, so, does he not intend to take your royal city?"*

The thought can be father to the action.

The very idea fueled Hanun's imagination. Readily persuaded that his advisers were right, he was convinced the delegation came as a cunning ploy to undermine his power.

In a drastic move that would have enormous repercussions all across David's powerful empire, Hanun took the peace ambassadors into custody. It was a serious breach of trust. More than that, he insulted them by the terrible twin indignities of shaving off half their beards and cutting off half their official robes at the buttocks.

For the Hebrew people this was the ultimate disgrace and most horrible humiliation. Their beards, so meticulously groomed, were a sign of virility, wisdom and manhood. Their long robes were worn with the utmost dignity to completely conceal and cover up their nakedness. Now both adornments were defiled.

In this uncouth condition David's emissaries were sent home in an act of despicable defiance. The news, when it reached David, enraged him. His men had been shamed! With enormous empathy for them he sent a swift courier to reassure them of his sympathy, suggesting they stay in the pleasant gardens and groves of Jericho until their clothing could be replaced and their luxuriant beards grew thick again.

Quickly word filtered back across the Jordan to Ammon that this rash act by Hanun had angered David to the point where the desert race literally stank in his estimation. Like so much putrifying trash he would bury them in their desert sands. At once they knew the Lion of Judah had been roused to attack them in a rampage of rage.

For not only Ammon, but also for all the erstwhile allies she would call to her aid, the end result would be huge costs in money and terrifying casualties in battle, far beyond anything they ever imagined. Just the false imagination of one man's mind would lead to loss, suffering, bloodshed and death for roughly sixty thousand men. One man's wrong thinking would precipitate a vicious war that would wipe out his people and reduce them to mere slaves in David's ever-growing empire.

This is a compelling commentary on the power and potential for evil that resides in the human intellect. Of all living creatures on the earth, only man has the peculiar and powerful capacity to actually *imagine* things which are not, as though they really do exist. Used in its proper and appropriate way, the imagination can be a gift from God which can be most creative. The finest art, the loftiest literature, the most moving music, the greatest architecture, the latest inventions began with birth in someone's inspired imagination.

Yet the same power, if not properly controlled by Christ, can be given over to the most insidious and destructive purposes. Instead of being used for uplifting and creative ends, it can drag one down into despicable behavior. It can distort thinking and give a false view of life. It can end in the indulgence of fantasies and self-deception that ultimately destroy the person.

Of course, Hanun was by no means a man whose mind was governed by God. The rash action and impulsive behavior of his imagination was to plunge his entire nation into terrible suffering, providing a classic example of how disastrous false imagination can be.

The Word of God speaks to this issue very emphatically. It gives us clear and categorical instructions as to how we should handle our imaginations. Unless brought under the control of Christ, they can readily become absolute monsters in our minds.

"For the weapons of our warfare are not carnal,
but mighty through God

> *to the pulling down of strongholds; (mental)*
> *casting down imaginations and every high thing*
> *that exalteth itself against the knowledge of God,*
> *and bringing into captivity every thought*
> *to the obedience of Christ"* (2 Corinthians 10:4-5).

If any man or woman is to be truly converted and born again, a profound change must be made in the mind. There simply must be formed in us the very mind of Christ. We must be transformed from character to character by His gracious Spirit through His Word. Only in this way do the standards, values and interests of Christ become ours by implicit obedience to Him.

In this way our imaginations are brought into line with His. Our thoughts are in accordance with His will. Our delight becomes the desire to please Him in positive ways.

In this particular case neither Hanun nor David were allowing their minds to be truly governed by God. For even in David's life he was allowing vengeance to replace justice for the insults heaped upon his emissaries.

Knowing that they would soon be attacked, Ammon sent to Syria, Zobah and Aram (Mesopotamia) for help. It will be recalled that these northern desert races were already subdued by David. They were vassal states under domination of Israel, controlled by garrisons stationed throughout the region. The situation was almost identical to the present-day domination of so-called Eastern Bloc countries of Europe by the U.S.S.R.

To elicit their help Ammon sent some forty-seven tons of silver bullion to the various desert chiefs to recruit mercenaries who would come and fight for them. This is roughly the equivalent of $9-10,000,000 in modern currency. Thus their fighting forces were increased substantially.

The two reports given of this engagement differ a great

deal in the numbers of horsemen, chariots and foot soldiers enlisted. The same applies to the final casualty lists at the end of the cruel war. One can only conclude that the records left to us were drawn up by two different reporters, one an infantry officer in David's army, the other a cavalry commander more interested in chariots and drivers.

Once more David turned to his ferocious and fearless commanding officer Joab to do the job of attacking Ammon and punishing them ruthlessly. At first it would appear that the monarch failed to realize that he faced a serious general insurrection in his empire of the nomadic northern races. It was thought this was a local skirmish that Joab could quickly settle.

When Joab joined battle with the enemy he was surprised to find that he had to fight on two fronts. He was brilliant enough and experienced enough in war to realize at once that his most formidable foe was the "army of Syrians" who were already in position outside the perimeter of Hanun's capital of Rabbah. There the fierce northern warriors and their cavalry units were prepared and waiting for Joab to attack Ammon.

In a swift and decisive military move, Joab divided his forces, pitting the most formidable men against the Syrians. The less experienced warriors he put under his brother Abishai to attack the Ammonites.

Joab was never short of self-assurance. Rough and tough, he lived with swagger and bravado. Bloodshed, war, battle, murder and mayhem were the warp and woof of his gory career. Yet here, for the first time, he seemed to sense that he had met his match in a struggle which could go either way.

He confided to his fearless brother Abishai that each should come to the aid of the other if the battle turned against them. He recognized that defeat was a distinct possibility. Even more astonishing, Joab actually elicits the favor of the Most High. Not that he ever exercised any personal faith in God, but he hoped vaguely that if he and Abishai fought like two unleashed lions Jehovah would smile on their valor and grant them victory.

With his usual dauntless courage Joab led his men against the Syrians in a brutal onslaught. The desert raiders were quickly routed and fled in fear. The Ammonites seeing their allies so rapidly vanquished fell back before Abishai and withdrew into the sanctuary of their fortified city. So the initial prospects seemed very promising and Joab returned home to Jerusalem flushed with victory.

But the Syrians were not done. Somehow they seemed to feel that by recruiting even more units from the north they could overthrow Israel's forces and break loose from their subjection to David. So cavalry units were recruited from even beyond the river Euphrates. Hordes of chariots, horses, and fierce drivers assembled for war. A major insurrection was under way! Now the whole of David's northern empire was in ferment ready for revolt.

No longer was this a localized skirmish with a few hot-headed desert brigands. David was astute enough to see that the situation was so serious he himself would have to take command of all Israel's huge standing army. They were immediately put on full alert and ordered into action against the revolting Syrians.

It was a formidable engagement. With his usual brilliance and incredible charisma David stormed into battle against the Syrians. Even though he lacked cavalry of his own David did not let this deter him. The result was an overwhelming victory for Israel. It was a day of tremendous triumph. A terrible toll was taken of the enemy forces. Hundreds of chariots were captured; thousands of drivers were slaughtered on the hot desert sands; and a grim total of roughly sixty thousand warriors lay dead or dying under the merciless sun, felled by the screaming swords of Israel.

The terrible loss of life was more than Syria could endure. Their leaders immediately sued for peace with Israel. Again they agreed to armistice terms that bound them into absolute servitude to David. He had crushed them completely and destroyed any designs they ever held for rebelling against him again.

For Ammon it meant they would now face Israel alone. Though defeated on the field of battle, they would withdraw into Rabbah.

For David it was a glorious triumph. He could return to Jerusalem and rest on his laurels.

9

David, Uriah and Bathsheba

David's crushing conquest of the Syrians may have been a stirring triumph for his empire, but it would lead to his own most ignominious defeat and disgrace as a man. Few, few, indeed are those who can handle success well. Power, prestige and prominence in almost any arena of life have the capacity to corrupt the individual, reducing reputation to ruin.

David was no exception to this principle of perversion.

Instead of leading his forces again into battle against Ammon, now entrenched within the forbidding fortified city of Rabbah—known today as the city of Amman, the capital of Jordan—David decided to take his ease at home in Jerusalem while Joab went to war.

David the formidable warrior who had killed the lion, the bear, Goliath, hundreds of Philistines and Syrians, would himself suddenly fall prey to his own delicate desires for ease, luxury and pleasure. He who in the heat of battle could discipline himself and his men for heroic exploits could not control the sinister cravings of his inner soul for personal self-gratification.

It is the very ancient story of the struggle that rages within the soul of man for supremacy of his spirit. Will he be governed by God or by greed? Will he submit to the sovereignty of God's Spirit or be dominated by his own passionate self-indulgence? Will he be controlled by the presence of the living God or taken captive by his own carnal nature?

Luxuriating in the grandeur of his palace, enjoying the adulation of a grateful nation and resting comfortably on the laurels of his heroic exploits, David little realized the peril which his success brought to him. He who now stood so tall would fall.

He would fall for the charming complexion and full-some figure of a magnificent young woman whom he noticed bathing and perfuming herself on a rooftop nearby. He was taking a little stroll in the high flat balcony of his own regal mansion when his gaze fell upon this gorgeous girl adorning herself in a nearby courtyard. Her remarkable beauty fascinated him. Never before, despite having numerous wives and concubines of his own, had he seen a woman quite as alluring.

It was not enough for him just to look.

It was not sufficient just to fantasize.

It was not his just to hope and dream and wish.

David had to have her!

First he would find out who she was. For though she was a neighbor, residing only a short distance from his regal palace, he did not know her. They must meet!

Word came back that she, Bath-sheba, belonged to another. She was, in fact, wife to Uriah, one of the most loyal and notable warriors in David's illustrious army. He was on combat duty, camped in the blazing desert sun with Joab outside the stern walls of Rabbah.

He would not be home for a long while!

This David knew full well. Was it pure chance that he should have such an open opportunity to summon Bath-sheba to the palace? Surely she could not refuse such an honor as to meet the monarch in person? What was his wish? Why invite her, who was wed to one who was not even an Israeli? Did he have some special honor to bestow upon her brave and heroic husband?

These and a thousand other questions must have coursed through the woman's excited emotions. Perhaps she little dreamed of the king's true desires. Fortunately for her, it was the most opportune time of the month to appear before his majesty. Her period was past. She could stand beautiful before the king purified, perfumed and robed in her most glamorous apparel.

The encounter was one of excruciating mutual attraction.

That night, at the peak of their passion, they mated—and she conceived.

Proudly, gladly, swiftly, Bath-sheba sent word back to David that she carried his child within her womb. She was sure he would be thrilled. What she did not understand was the enormous spiritual crisis into which her lover had been plunged. She was a pagan woman, a stranger to the laws of the Lord. How could she comprehend?

For David the hour of deepening darkness had come! Step by step in ever-descending degradation he would turn to the most diabolical decisions to try and erase his steps of sin. Each succeeding action was more awful than the one before it. He was literally descending into a black dungeon of self-imprisonment. He was being shackled by his own sins. And in the dreadful darkness of those days, he was acutely aware that he had estranged himself from the Most High.

Yet there seemed no turning back!

In his passion he had forgotten the presence of God!

In his self-indulgence he had sinned grievously against the gracious, gentle Spirit of the Lord, who loved him!

What David had done was much more than adultery. It was more than seducing a magnificent woman. It was more than giving full play to his urgent male passions.

He had sinned against God, who in such compassion and concern had accompanied him all the days of his life. He had wounded and grieved the Spirit of God who had guided him so surely for so many years. He had rebelled against Jehovah, God very God, Christ very Christ, who resided within his soul and made it His sanctuary.

Added to all of this anguish he had wronged this lovely lady. He had prostituted her beauty to his own selfish purposes. He had double-crossed and utterly betrayed one of his fighting men. Uriah was one of David's most loyal warriors. This shattered their confidence in him. He had sinned against himself in the agony of destroying his own self-respect and thus crushing his own self-esteem (*see Proverbs 6:32*).

David was in the depths of despair! And he was desperate!

In his extremity he tried to extricate himself. He would use cunning and intrigue to cover his steps. He sent orders at once for Uriah to report to him about the battle for Rabbah. The illustrious fighter would welcome a few days of leave at home. It would be a treat to have a break from the battle lines. And, what could be better than a few nights of rest in the comfort of his own bed, relishing the loveliness of his beautiful wife?

Thus, it would be assumed, that any child born by Bathsheba had been fathered by her rightful husband. So the illicit affair would go unnoticed.

Quite obviously David did not know Uriah well. Nor did he count on the steel-firm sturdiness of this gallant man's devotion to duty. Little did David ever dream that a Hittite of Canaanite extraction could demonstrate such remarkable loyalty to the king himself, to Joab his commanding officer, and to his comrades in arms, even though most were Hebrews.

After giving a full report of the siege of Rabbah to David, the monarch, Uriah was dismissed with clear instructions to go home, refresh himself and take his ease. This he refused to do. Instead he chose to sleep in full battle gear at the gate of the royal palace, guarding its entrance through the long night watches.

When this noble action was reported to David he promptly summoned the stalwart warrior to appear before him again. "Why didn't you go home and relax after coming back so far from battle?"

Uriah's reply was a stabbing rebuke to the comfortable king. "Dare I go to luxuriate in the comfort of my home and make love to my beautiful wife when the Ark of God, my commander Joab, and my comrades in arms are camped in open peril facing the enemy? I would never do this disgraceful deed!"

It was a shock to David! Such a noble man! Such a sterling character!

Since David's first gentle suggestion to Uriah that he quietly go home and take his ease, did not work, the faltering king decided on more desperate measures. He had set his feet on a slippery downward path that became ever more repulsive. He ordered the loyal warrior to spend still another day in Jerusalem. That night he would wine and dine Uriah in great honor at his own royal banqueting table.

As the evening wore on David plied the man with more and more wine until he was thoroughly drunk. The monarch's empty hope was that the poor, intoxicated fellow would stagger home in a stupor to lie with the beautiful Bath-sheba in his own warm bed.

But David was dealing with no ordinary lout from the rough ranks of his army. He was mired deeply in his own wretched intrigue of trying to use a valiant, loyal warrior to cover his own sinister sins. Uriah was not to be manipulated, even when inebriated. His profound sense of duty to his comrades, to his adopted country and to his king demanded that he again sleep with the other watchmen at the gate of the king's residence.

What a tangled web of duplicity David now devised. Almost in horror we recoil from his sinister schemes. He descends even deeper into cruel chicanery.

In desperation David decides to have the man destroyed who shows such unflinching loyalty to him. The thought alone troubles our spirits and enrages our sensibilities of honor and decency. It seems beyond our comprehension that this shepherd of the Most High, this composer of such exquisite music, this poet of such profound psalms, this monarch, so great an empire builder, this statesman of such justice in administration, could suddenly sink to the depths of a cold, grim, calculating murderer.

But he did!

And the method his convoluted mind contrived shatters us!

David decided to use Uriah's own fierce loyalty and

unflinching valor in battle to destroy the man in action. In haste he scribbled an order to Joab, that the tough commander place Uriah in the very forefront of the attack on Rabbah. This would put him in a position of greatest peril beneath the enemy walls where he was bound to be killed when Joab deliberately withdrew support from him.

Adding insult to injury David dared to seal the orders, handed them to Uriah in person and commanded that the dear fellow carry his own death warrant back to Joab in the battle zone. It was a dastardly deed! It makes us despise David's action with profound loathing! This was a level of disloyalty far greater than the most vicious behavior of brute beasts. It was merciless and brutal, yet done with such smooth, insidious subtlety.

One cannot help but ponder what the outcome might have been had Uriah dared to open the letter, if but for an instant he had set aside his loyalty to the king and broken the seal to read the royal orders. The whole course of Israel's empire might have changed in an hour. In the white heat of his flaming anger, Uriah might easily have returned to rush at the king and use his valiant sword to sever the royal head. It would not be the first time a monarch was murdered. David's very life and the entire future of his nation dangled on the slim thread of Uriah's unwavering loyalty.

The two men stand before us in blazing contrast. The foreign Hittite so faithful to the very end. The cunning king so caught in dishonorable intrigue of his own making.

The Spirit of the living God, in portraying the lives of God's people, makes no attempt to mask their dark blemishes of character. With bold strokes he paints them before our astonished gaze exactly as they are. He never covers over the corruption of the human heart. He shows us what we are!

It might well seem to us at this point that David now was indeed beyond redemption. Certainly for the casual reader with little if any spiritual understanding this episode in the king's life removes him from any further possibility of human respect. The inescapable verdict would seem to be one of absolute abhorrence—especially for one who claimed to honor the Most High. Certainly David's duplicity has brought endless reproach upon the man, and upon all of God's people, across the ensuing centuries.

As we shall see in the next chapter only the grace of God and the unfailing faithfulness of His Spirit, still at work in David's life, could ever lift him again from the deep and terrible pit of evil in which he was mired.

The ruthless, rough, tough, hard-headed Joab tore open the letter handed to him by the weary Uriah. Without blinking an eye in disbelief, without showing a single emotion of revulsion, without a moment's hesitation, he calmly crumpled it up in his bloodstained hands and ordered Uriah into the forefront of the battle lines.

In cold, cruel compliance with David's demands, Joab became an active co-conspirator in Uriah's death. Not for a second did he debate the issue within himself. Being a party to this murder of an innocent man would give Joab the grim leverage of blackmail over the king for the rest of his days.

What both Joab and David clearly forgot is that any secret shared by two people is no longer a secret—only is it such if one of them is dead. And sooner or later all the dreadful details of this ghastly story would be common knowledge all across the country. Nor was God Himself silent or oblivious to the horrendous harm done to Is-

rael. Soon the whole nation would know of this great
wickedness.

Exactly as planned, Uriah was killed in action against
the Ammonites. For this to happen, not only he but many
of his loyal comrades had to fall in a futile assault against
the city.

Joab feared David might be enraged when he heard
of the heavy casualties. Still he suspected that when the
messenger informed the king the heavy losses were offset
by Uriah's death, all would be well. Joab was sure, somehow, that the loyal warrior's demise was of greater consequence to David just now, than any loss of other lives,
or even defeat beneath the brutal city walls of Rabbah.
In a cruel, taunting way Joab reminded David that an
angry woman had killed Abimelech with a piece of mill-
stone. Perhaps he, too, now stood in great peril, trapped
by the allurements of a beautiful woman in the background of his life.

David, relieved at last that the awful deed had been
done, replied to Joab that he need not be dismayed by
the loss of his valiant men. After all, it was part of the
ebb and flow of war to lose some and gain some. If necessary he should regroup his forces and fight even more
ferociously to subdue Ammon.

Meanwhile, word came to Bath-sheba that her heroic
husband had been killed in battle. As was the custom
she immediately went into mourning for her man.
Whether or not it was genuine grief she expressed is difficult to determine. Perhaps the passionate flame of her
new love had already extinquished the former affection
she held for Uriah. Who knows?

Certainly she did not hesitate to respond quickly to
David's invitation to become his wife when her mourning
period was passed. In a bold and brazen way the king

proceeded at once to legitimatize their union by taking her into his already substantial harem. It was a clever ploy which may have satisfied the niceties of his culture. It may well have seemed his royal perogative to do this even though he had plotted her magnificent husband's death.

But the thing David had done displeased the LORD!

10

God Disciplines David

The despicable things David had done may have seemed to be covered over by his cunning, screened from view by his subtlety. But they were not hidden from God! The gracious Spirit of the Most High, whose residence was in this man, was deeply grieved. The person of the living Lord Jehovah who had been David's constant companion was wounded by the wickedness.

For in fact and in grim reality, David had sinned grievously against God, not only in his own life, but also in the life of Bath-sheba; in the life of Uriah; in the life of Joab; in the life of the whole nation of Israel.

The appalling result was that the enemies of God, and there have been millions of them over thousands of years, would ridicule and blaspheme The Eternal One because of the misdeeds of this one man. The honor, the name, the grandeur of God our Father would be dragged into the dust by this disgusting episode.

I recall vividly the day when I sat in a literature lecture and heard my instructor read this account. Closing the pages with a sharp smack he glared out through his glasses at us teen-age students and growled angrily: "If that is the sort of thing God's people do, I don't even want to hear about Him!" It was a vicious indictment that devastated me.

So it was, too, in David's day.

God could not remain silent.

He had to take drastic steps to discipline the offender.

Nathan, the prophet, was sent to David with a burning message.

It was the second time Nathan came with courage, prepared to confront David with sobering news. He was wise enough to speak in parable form. This is the most potent mode of expression used in primitive societies. It was the means of communication used by Jesus to convey spiritual truth to tough people. It was like holding up a mirror before the soul of man in which to see one's true self.

The touching story is well known. A poor man had a tiny pet lamb which was his most precious possession. He had reared it lovingly by hand along with his own children until it was like a member of the family.

In the same town there lived a very wealthy man. When unexpected visitors came to his house he refused to take even one lamb from his huge flocks. Instead by sheer perfidy he seized the poor man's pet, had it slaughtered, then served it as a feast to his guests.

The parable sent David into a rage: *"As the LORD lives, that man must die!"* And, he went on to shout angrily, *"He must restore the lamb four times over because he had no pity!"*

With unflinching eyes the brave prophet looked at David's flushed face and spoke in level tones:

96

God Disciplines David

"You are the man!"

It was as if this mighty monarch of so majestic an empire had been struck between the eyes with a sword. It was indeed that! It was the sword of the Word of the living God that stabbed deep into his soul, into his spirit, into his quivering conscience.

Clearly, sharply, painfully, he saw himself in the awfulness of his horrendous evil. *"He had no pity!"*

In his arrogance, haughtiness and power David had selfishly exploited Bath-sheba in brazen adultery.

In his covetousness and cold-blooded callousness, he had planned the death of Uriah—outright murder.

In his self-centered preoccupation, he had deliberately implicated Joab in his crime and false accusation.

In his sin against God and man, David had brought obscene blasphemy upon His honor.

For any single one of these offenses he deserved to die. This was stated clearly in the Levitical laws, which he knew and understood so well (see: Leviticus 20:10 & 24:16–17).

David stood in death! He stood condemned! He stood in mortal peril of being pulverized to powder by the inviolate laws of God which he had ignored and transgressed with such proud impunity! It is always so with anyone who despises the Most High and disregards His will and wishes.

Only, only, only the redemptive mercy, the incredible pity, the eternal generosity of a compassionate, caring, loving, merciful God could possibly forgive his offenses.

This David saw!

This he now knew!

This he understood as his only hope!

He was utterly silent, subdued, smitten before Nathan.

He who had no pity on others, now cast himself on the eternal, bountiful pity of Jehovah God.

The anguish of soul, the agony of spirit, the acute pain of David's whole poetic being at this point is poured out in Psalm 51:1–2.

"Have mercy upon me, O God, according to thy loving kindness: according unto the multitude of thy tender mercies blot out my transgressions. Wash me thoroughly from mine iniquity and cleanse me from my sin!"

Such a cry of confession finds a ready response with God. Such profound repentance as poured from David's spirit was sure to touch the redemptive heart of the Most High. Such brokenness was bound to be healed. Such admission of sin was the way to forgiveness and restoration.

Yet one terrible truth remained. One profound principle of divine discipline would endure. One awesome penalty had to be paid. *"What a man sows he reaps."*

For, though David was forgiven his offenses and his life spared from immediate death, he would have to endure the severe consequences of his evil actions for the rest of his days. He would be chastened, rebuked, corrected and disciplined severely for his wrongs.

It was the inevitable out-working of the inviolate laws of God. Modern man calls it "cause and effect." Our Father God sees it as a benevolent act of His own amazing grace to the willful, wayward sons of men. *"For whom the LORD loveth He chasteneth, and scourgeth every son whom he receiveth"* (Hebrews 12:6).

The prophet, Nathan, speaking under the unction and direction of God's Spirit, made no bones about this severe consequence for David. It was not that God was vindictive. He would simply discipline and chasten this one who had despised Him and ignored His precepts. He did it because of His enormous compassion and concern for the shattered man.

Nathan reminded David that it was God, very God, who had given him everything he possessed. All his wealth, power, influence, wives, family, reputation, skills and empire came as outright gifts from the generous hands of a gracious living God. He as a mere man had no single reason to be proud, haughty or arrogant. Nor do any of us mere mortals. None of us are "self-made men or women." That is a travesty of truth, the evil product of man's innate pride.

In short, stabbing syllables the bold prophet went on to warn David that the penalty for his pride would be most painful. For the rest of his life, about twenty more years, he would taste appalling bloodshed, war, intrigue and conspiracy.

Much of the awful mayhem and sorrow David would endure for the rest of his days would emerge from his own family and among his own offspring. The king would be humbled by his own household; brought to the dust of despair by his cruel, crafty sons; made to taste some of the same terrible atrocities in public that he himself had perpetrated in private.

Lastly the child conceived by Bath-sheba out of wedlock would die.

When Nathan left the presence of the king it was as if a great stillness of somber solemnity descended on the palace. David had not debated the issues with the prophet. He was too wise, too spiritually sensitive to the word of God's Spirit, to offer excuses for his atrocious acts.

That stillness was soon followed by the whimpering

cries of Bath-sheba's child. A severe illness gripped the wee lad. David knew at once that the prophet's prediction was coming to pass. That, in fact, was the proof positive that he was indeed, and in truth, a prophet. His was a sure word from the Lord.

Amid his anguish of soul David prostrated himself on the floor beside the child's bed. He fasted and pled earnestly for the boy to be restored. For an entire week he did this, imploring the Most High to restore the youngster to health.

All to no avail!

On the surface it may have seemed a noble action.

In truth it was a case of self-gratification.

If the boy had been healed and grown to manhood, he would have borne the dreadful stigma of a bastard all his life. In that society to be an illegitimate child was to be a marked person of low esteem all one's days.

David seemed to forget this awful aspect completely. It was in fact a great mercy that God took the wee lad when He did. It was an act of compassion to spare the child so much emotional suffering.

For David, too, it was fortunate that Jehovah would not give him his own way again. As pointed out so clearly in *David I*, it is a most dangerous thing to demand things from God. We insist on having our own way at great peril to ourselves. Sometimes God allows men and women to gain their own ends, with disastrous consequences.

As soon as David's servants alerted him that the child had died, he rose, changed his attire, washed, anointed himself and went at once to the tabernacle. It seemed odd!

But it was not! It was appropriate and proper that he, the king, should there give thanks and worship in integrity. True worship for God's person is not necessarily some special singing of songs, raising of hands or chanting *"Praise the LORD."*

Genuine worship implies that in any event of life, no matter how trying, the worshiper complies implicitly with God's will and wishes. This is done in three deliberate steps.

1) *Acknowledge*—oh, God, you are God, well able to arrange all the details of life for my well-being.

2) *Accept*—all such arrangements without debate. In this way peace comes. The soul is at rest.

3) *Approve*—of all that God does. Give thanks with genuine gratitude no matter how grievous the situation.

It was in this spirit that David worshiped. He knew the wee lad had gone to glory. He knew too that because he himself had been redeemed from his sin he would join him. Most important, by his true worship he freed God's great hands to move on his behalf as a man forgiven and made whole.

In this new dimension of spiritual strength and life David could comfort, console and go in again to Bath-sheba in renewed energy. Again she bore a beautiful, handsome boy. They named him *Solomon* (*the peaceable one*) for all was at peace between them and God.

Even more astonishing was the arrival of Nathan again. This time he brought the most beautiful news imaginable. It was a brief, ecstatic, explosive word of good cheer from the Lord God. *"I have called your son—Jedidiah—meaning, He is beloved of the LORD!"*

This one would be a special man for special service!

What a consolation to David and Bath-sheba!

Surely, surely, only the God of all grace could lift them from the dark depths of utter degradation to the bright light of His love.

Such is the mercy of the Most High! Such is the pity

with which our Father pitieth His children when they repent and seek His face.

As if to put the final seal of His approbation upon David after his spiritual renewal, God saw fit to grant the monarch another major military victory. Though David had, long ago, defeated and subdued the Syrians who had come to Ammon's aid, the latter remained strongly entrenched in the stronghold of Rabbah.

Joab, surly, tough and undaunted as any commander could be, had failed to breach the fortified defenses of this desert city. Finally, however, the furious commander decided to try and take the head waters that supplied the royal city of Rabbah. In this he succeeded, and it was not unlike the strategy used to storm Jerusalem when he was the first to ascend into the fortress through the underground water tunnels.

He immediately sent word to David that he had taken the water supply. It was only a matter of days until the desperate people, deprived of water in Rabbah, would surrender. As a noble gesture of loyalty to the king he urged him to come at once and capture the defenders, garnering the honor for the final triumph.

It was probably the most generous move ever made by Joab. In part it may have been his crude military way of showing David that despite his recent spiritual humiliation, he still respected the monarch as a military genius.

David seized the city, captured the king, dethroned him and placed the mighty gold crown, worth at least one quarter of a million dollars today, on his own head. Besides this there was enormous booty and huge spoils of war which would be carried back to Jerusalem. Part of it would be set aside for the tabernacle treasury. It was a tremendous triumph.

God Disciplines David

The nation of Ammon, like its allies, were brought into the empire as a subject people. They were put to work hewing timber, cultivating crops, building bricks, just as Israel, so long before, had been slaves to the pharaohs of Egypt.

In majesty, power and great honor David and his army returned to Jerusalem as radiant victors.

11

Evil and Violence within David's Own Family

The second calamity to engulf David, as foretold by Nathan, was the eruption of great evil within his own family. This would lead to violence, mayhem and murder among his own offspring. His family would be fractured and eventually he himself would be deposed from power by the outright rebellion of Absalom, his third son.

The awful consequences of his wrongs against Uriah, Bath-sheba and Joab would dog his footsteps until the very end of his days. He would know sorrow upon sorrow and shed tears upon tears until he longed to be taken from the earth.

It all began in what appeared to be a rather harmless way. His eldest, firstborn son, Amnon, rightful heir to his throne and first prince in his royal family, became utterly infatuated with his half-sister, Tamar. She was a gorgeous girl, full sister to Absalom, who was born to David's wife Maacah, a pagan princess from Geshur in Syria.

So intense was Amnon's passion for the beautiful Tamar that it quite literally made him ill. This was much more than mere "puppy-love." It was a consuming desire that demanded fulfillment even though Amnon understood its evil in Israel.

Unfortunately Amnon had an erstwhile friend, Jonadab, actually one of his cousins, who suggested in a sinister way how Tamar might be trapped and exploited for Amnon's own ends. Being a crafty, cruel fellow, he whispered to Amnon that he was sure the king himself could be counted on to feel sorry for his son and so send Tamar to care for him when he feigned serious illness in his home.

Surely David would not be averse to allowing his lovely Tamar to tend the bedside of her brother. She could be invited to prepare the poor fellow some delicacies that would lift his spirits and restore his strength. Just having her close to him would bring such good cheer!

Strange and incredulous as it may seem to us, the king fell for the ruse. He seemed ever ready to indulge the whims of his sons. As later events were to disclose, David simply would not discipline his children. It was to prove one of his greatest weaknesses as a father. Perhaps punishment for wrong was too drastic for his poetic temperament. More likely, like most soft parents, he was afraid to alienate the affections of his offspring. The price for proper conduct was too high for him to pay.

In any event, complying weakly with Amnon's request, David ordered Tamar to tend her brother's needs. This she had every right to refuse. After all she was a royal princess in Israel. And royal princesses did not do menial service nor submit themselves to the lowly household duties of preparing meals and serving the sick.

But the beautiful young woman went in obedience to her father's wishes. Obviously she was more than beautiful in body but also generous in spirit and gracious in personality to respond so readily to one in need. She was well named—*the palm*—that brought beauty and blessing wherever she stood.

What she did not seem to see was that she was walking straight into a trap prepared so craftily by her cousin and her half-brother. For when she had prepared the dainties for Amnon and brought them to his bedside he grabbed her forcibly in attempt to seduce her. He had ordered all his servants from the house so now he was alone, flushed, ready to rape the trembling girl, if need be.

Tamar cried out for his compassion. She literally flung herself on his nonexistent mercy. She offered to become his legitimate wife and bride if only he would request his father for her hand. She reminded him of the awful sin and shame incest would bring into their royal family and into the nation. It would be an act of utter folly and dreadful degradation.

Amnon was deaf to her pleas.

In passion and heat he seized her violently and raped her by brute force.

Amnon would have fitted comfortably into our soft, permissive, corrupt Western world of the late twentieth century. He was a selfish young person determined to indulge his own lascivious desires no matter how much damage and despair it brought to others. He was a typical product so characteristic of the "me" generation. His only motto in life was that of our modern society, *"If it feels good—just do it!"*

People both within the church and outside of it seem to be puzzled by the fragmentation of the family. A thousand so-called wise psychologists and even more learned psychiatrists pontificate at length about all the reasons for the wreckage in society. They write ten thousand books about the subject and offer as many lectures to line their own pockets on the pain of a perishing civilization.

Yet it can all be summed up in a single sentence: *"The heart [will] of man is deceitful [selfish] and desperately wicked. Who can know [fathom] it?"* (Jeremiah 17:9).

Our much admired media, our theaters, our publishers, our professors and educators, our novelists and journalists all pander to the putrid. They glamorize promiscuity. Even some preachers ardently promote self-love in the name of positive thinking and pseudo-Christianity.

Is it any wonder that our sophisticated society has spawned ten million *Amnons?* Is it surprising that womanhood has been exploited and ravaged so ruthlessly? Are we astonished to see the explosive reaction in the eruption and corruption of feminine liberation movements?

It is imperative that pastors should be brave enough to confront men who willfully, selfishly, ruthlessly exploit beautiful girls just as Amnon did. Who dare to toss them aside as so much soiled trash. It is a terrible travesty—a blot on our proud society.

What Amnon did was to destroy Tamar.

Not only had he raped her physically.

He had also ruined her emotionally.

And he had plunged her into a prison of deep despair.

Though she went from his rooms garbed in glowing gowns of multicolored hues, she went with a broken will to live, a shattered spirit. On her lovely hair, so thick and lustrous like her brother Absalom's, she sprinkled ashes rather than wear her diamond tiara. Her dignity as a glorious virgin had been stripped and stolen from her by a selfish, crude man. She (*the palm*) had been through a violent tornado of pain and shame that left her beaten and broken.

She walked now as one dead, in disgrace, yet in fact alive among men who could scarcely comprehend her inner anguish. Once so beautiful! Now so battered! Once so attractive! Now so despised!

Absalom, her handsome brother, so proud, so pagan, so self-preoccupied, had small comfort for his weeping sister. He appeared almost totally insensitive to her searing agony. All he cared about really was that this act of violence against his sister would provide him with an excuse to wreak terrible revenge on Amnon. For the present he was too weak, too cowardly, too contriving to face the crude fellow and confront him with his terrible sin against men and God.

Meanwhile Amnon discreetly tried to reassure Tamar that the deed really was not so dastardly—after all he was her half-brother. The suggestion alone was loathsome.

As for David, his attitude was one of furious anger and burning outrage. Yet he, too, remained silent. He would not, indeed, he could not condemn his son, the first prince in the kingdom. He dare not even try to discipline his heir apparent.

Why? Because his own hands were stained with the blood of Uriah. His own position was compromised by the affair with Bath-sheba. He stood impotent to act.

Because of this lack of action against Amnon, young Absalom hated both his brother (who had raped his sister) and also his father, David. With a burning passion he despised both of them and so began to plot their overthrow. Ultimately he would decide to destroy Amnon, and later lay careful, cruel plans to rebel against his father and usurp his throne in open revolt.

There can be no doubt Absalom partially implicated his father in Tamar's disgrace, especially since it was he who sent her to wait on Amnon. So Absalom held the king responsible for the reproach that fell on his family.

Lastly Absalom had looked for some stern sort of discipline from David in correcting his elder brother. It was not forthcoming. Quite logically, he concluded that likewise there would be none on him if he took violence into his own hands to avenge himself on Amnon. His pagan background enabled him not only to despise the laws of the Lord, but even more immediately to despise his own father with deep loathing.

Herein lay the explanation for all his subsequent evil.

Two long years he waited in sullen silence for a chance to destroy Amnon. Two long years he banked the hot fires of his hatred against David. Two long years he schemed craftily how he could seize the kingdom.

At last his hour of reprisal had come. He was having a festive celebration to mark the end of the shearing season among his flocks. There would be a gala banquet. The wine would flow freely and all the royal sons of the royal household, far from home, could throw off their usual restraints in the sun-drenched pastures of Ephraim.

Absalom even invited David to come. Perhaps his original black-hearted plan was to murder both his father and brother in one fell swoop of his sword. But the king declined his son's invitation. He insisted it would be too great a burden for his boy to bear. Still he blessed him for his generous gesture.

Ever anxious to indulge Absalom and curry his favor, David consented to let all his sons accompany Absalom to the shearing festival. Somehow, deep down, David must have had some premonition that all was not well. Still he was too weak-willed to cross his strong-willed son.

Each of the princes mounted his own mule and rode off bravely to the banquet. Little did any of them realize the risk they ran. For as soon as the celebration was well under way and Amnon was thoroughly intoxicated with strong wine Absalom commanded his servants to rush in and murder him on the spot.

In stark terror the other princes each rushed from the ghastly scene. They leaped into their royal saddles and dashed off for Jerusalem on their mules.

This was the second occasion on which the royal household had used wine to achieve wicked designs. The first time was when David had hoped the drunken Uriah would go home to lie with Bath-sheba and so cover his own crime against her. Now David's son was using the fermented drink to commit this terrible crime.

Despite all the specious arguments advanced within the church, based on a few random passages, that the use of wine and liquor is acceptable behavior for God's people, the evidence is to the contrary. Broken homes, fractured families, child abuse, shattered careers, battered women, destitute homes, ruined lives, highway deaths, all attest to the awful folly of drinking. The cost to contemporary society of this addiction is beyond calculation. Yet for the most part the contemporary church remains silent on the subject. Weak-kneed pastors are unwilling to warn their people of the awful perils they face in the use of alcohol.

Amnon little knew that day that he would die a drunk. Not even his hapless friend Jonadab, though aware of the plot, had cared enough to warn him. He, too, was

in his cups. All of them together were more stupid than
the mules they rode.

The first news of Absalom's atrocity which came back
to David in Jerusalem was exaggerated. It was reported
that all his sons were slain. The terrible message undid
David. The king tore off his royal tunic and flung himself
face down on the earth in mourning.

Soon other messengers came bearing more reliable
news that only Amnon, the heir apparent, had been
wiped out. The other younger princes had all escaped
and were riding home. Absalom, meanwhile, in the midst
of the mayhem had fled and made good his escape back
to the region of his mother's pagan people. He would
take refuge in Geshur among the Syrians where he felt
fairly safe.

It is remarkable indeed that not one of the other
princes had sufficient courage or iron in their spine to
confront Absalom in a counterattack. It is even more astonishing that David in the face of such a cold-blooded
murder did not dispatch a contingent of his ferocious
fighting men to Geshur to bring Absalom back to justice.
Geshur lay within his empire. It was a part of the vassal
state of Syria. He had it well within his power to see
that his son was brought before the law of the Lord. It
might well have saved the young man's soul.

Instead the king turned to mourning. He was living
in a dreadful form of daily death. It was precisely what
the prophet Nathan had foretold would happen to his
family. It is odd David mourned the death of Amnon
only briefly, as if he was of little account. Yet he yearned
desperately for Absalom. The make-up of man is so convoluted no one can explain it.

What we do know is that David's disregard for some

of God's solemn edicts was now producing unrelieved pain in his life. He had taken pagan wives. He himself had been an adulterer and murderer. He had failed to discipline either himself or his sons under the great hand of God. He neglected to correct his children. He had not grounded them carefully in the laws of the Lord. And because he was so busy with the affairs of state his priorities were reversed and in disarray (See Deuteronomy 6:3–15).

12

Joab Contrives for Absalom to Return to Jerusalem

For reasons not given to us in the Scriptures, David yearned fiercely for his absent son Absalom. He had many other children by his numerous wives and assorted concubines. So why the king's special affection should have been focused on this one wayward son is rather difficult to determine.

Perhaps he saw in the handsome young man a replica of himself. Perhaps his secret hope was that the headstrong young prince might one day become a mighty man of God. Or it may have been that this constant pining was the unbridled grief of a father's affection for his son.

Joab was troubled enough by the king's behavior that he decided steps should be taken to return the exile. It has to be remembered, of course, that it was Absalom who in terror of his life had voluntarily returned to live in Geshur among the Syrians. He had not been banished by David. In actual fact David had never even spoken a word of correction to the young criminal, much less taken any action to bring him to justice for murdering Amnon.

Three years had now elapsed since Absalom fled. They were long and trying years. Joab was fed up with David's constant despair. Being a thoroughly pragmatic person he contrived to use a wise woman in Tekoah to trap David and force him into a reconciliation with the estranged prince. Beyond restoring the family ties, Joab no doubt felt sure his wily scheme would win favor for himself both with David and the young Absalom. How wrong he was! Just the opposite would happen!

The wise woman who agreed to Joab's scheme really was an intelligent lady willing to try to help the king in a devious way. But she was far from wise in allowing herself to be persuaded to act out a lie in trapping the monarch.

She came before David seeking a special audience with him. She claimed she was a widow with two sons. The boys, while working in the fields, got into a fierce dispute. In the heat of their differences one killed the other. Now the entire family demanded that justice be done. The surviving son should pay with his life, under the ancient law of "blood for blood."

Her plea was that if this was done, she would be left utterly destitute. No one remained to care for her or to carry on the family name. More than that, she would be quenched like the last glowing ember of a dying fire.

With his poetic temperament and artistic nature David was deeply moved by the woman's impassioned plea. Obviously she was a consummate actress and played her part to perfection. Joab had chosen well. Perhaps he should have elected to be a drama producer rather than a military commander at this pivotal point in his stormy career. Certainly his life would have been much less stormy in the future.

So deeply was David touched by the woman's story

that he did not pause to reflect carefully on just what the prudent course of action should be. As king in Israel he was not permitted of God to be a royal despot or cruel tyrant the way Saul had been. Under Moses, clear and explicit guidelines had been laid down for Israel exactly how a king should rule in judicial matters (read carefully Deuteronomy 17:8–20).

Israel was always seen to be governed by God, not by man. So even if a king eventually came to power, his responsibility before the people was to take crucial matters of justice to the priests in the tabernacle, who, with the judges there, would seek God's guidance. The ultimate divine decision would be given to the king. Thus justice would be served.

This David neglected to do. Unlike that great and godly hero of old, Joshua, who worked so closely with Eleazer the High Priest, David simply bypassed the "chain of command" arranged by the Most High. He set the law of the Lord aside and waived the responsibility of carrying out his royal duties before the people.

He had done this in failing to discipline Amnon for the rape of his sister Tamar. He had done this in failing to bring Absalom to justice for the murder of his brother Amnon. Now again he took the law into his own hands and promised the woman from Tekoah that no harm would befall her son guilty of murdering his brother.

In truth what was happening in David's life, and, for that matter, in his family and in the kingdom, was a dangerous breakdown of law and order. Offenders were not being brought to trial. The most heinous crimes were being openly committed without serious consequences to the offenders. Justice simply was not being served the way it should be.

Not only was this a most dangerous drift in David's

own personal life. It also meant that evil men within the nation could carry out their crimes with impunity simply because they knew they were immune from paying the penalty for their misdeeds.

Of course, it may be argued that David could scarcely have been expected to carry out the appropriate death penalty on Absalom his son. The awful truth of the matter is that the same end result would work out in his life with horrendous sorrow and suffering for the rest of his days. In his arrogance and pride, Absalom would consider himself "above the law." He would disregard the edicts of the Most High with impunity. He assured himself he could do as he pleased because his father would never cross or correct him.

Deliberately, brazenly, he would break the laws of God.

In turn, but too late, he would discover those same laws could crush him!

Just as soon as David promised the woman that her guilty son would be given complete asylum and allowed to go free, she pressed the point home with David—"Then why don't you do the same for your own son Absalom?"

At once the monarch saw he had been trapped. Like a bird in a snare, he was caught in the web of his own wrongdoing. At once he discerned that it was Joab, behind the scenes, who had put him into this impossible position. Despite all of his prowess and prestige with his people, the king had been duped by this scheme.

It seemed to the beleaguered David that he really had no other option but to send Joab to bring Absalom back to Jerusalem. It appeared any choice he made now would only serve to drive him deeper into difficulty with his own son. Even more disagreeable was the realization that in this case he really was not in charge. It was the rough, tough, ruthless Joab who was manipulating him like a mere pawn on the chessboard of his own game plan.

As we look on it, it is difficult not to feel a certain compassion for David. Our natural human instincts are inclined to sympathize with his sufferings. Somehow we can readily identify with his inner struggle to try and please God yet not alienate his own family. We admit that we, too, under similar circumstances might well have made the same choices as he did.

But that simply was not a solution to his dilemma.

It did not satisfy the justice of God.

Nor did it meet the deep need for discipline in his son.

What he did was wrong in every way.

And it was evil simply because David failed to seek God's will.

Joab, on the other hand, was elated to think he could prevail over the king so easily. In false humility he prostrated himself on the ground before David, pretending to be subservient. All the time he gloated inwardly over his crafty success.

His self-applause would not last long!

He sped off to Geshur to fetch Absalom. No doubt he treated the prince with the utmost respect and decorum. After all, one day he might need this young fellow to further his own ends and feather his own nest a little more comfortably. Little did Joab realize he was not bringing home a kitten, but a terrible tiger.

While Joab was away on his supposed mission of mercy, David must have reconsidered his rash and hasty decision to have Absalom brought back. As a compromise measure, to assuage his troubled conscience, he decided not to see Absalom at all. The prince would live in his own handsome house in Jerusalem, but the two men would never meet face to face, never speak, never come to any sort of reconciliation. In other words, David decided to treat his son as if he was indeed dead. He would act as though justice had been done and the murderer had paid the supreme price with his own life. For Absalom it would be like a living death!

The whole episode must have been an absolute conundrum to the royal city. Tongues tattled. Gossip was rampant. And ten thousand tantalizing questions went unanswered. The most important by far was, *"Why the stand-off, the silence, between father and son?"*

For two long, terrible, tormenting years the impasse went on, neither monarch nor prince yielding an inch of ground. The king would be busy with all the affairs of state—presiding over royal functions and sumptuous banquets, meeting foreign ambassadors and emissaries, dealing out justice of some sort to his own people in their perplexity.

As for Absalom, there was little for him to do but play the part of a royal "playboy," a veritable idle drone in his father's domain. With his regal appearance, his magnificent physique and handsome head of hair he would be a favorite in the social life of the glittering city. But it was not enough for one with his temper and his ambitions.

The day was approaching when he must act!

If the monarch would not come to him, then he would come to the monarch.

To do this he was even willing to jeopardize the well-being of his whole family. By now he had four children of his own, three boys and one gorgeous girl whom he named Tamar. The name was a constant reminder of his beautiful sister, the girl's aunt, who had been raped by Amnon. Never, never, never would Absalom allow himself to forget the initial evil that led to Amnon's death. Since his father had failed to execute justice on his eldest brother, he had waited two years, then did the dreadful deed himself. Blood had been spilled to expiate the awful wrong against his family.

Now his family was being wronged again. In his pagan pride and haughty heart he saw himself as innocent of any wrong. He had a right to see the king, to seek some kind of reconciliation. He had a right to be either pardoned or punished. But the silence had to end!

Twice Absalom sent his servants to Joab asking that the commander come to see him. He was sure Joab was the only person in Israel who could prevail on David to see him, his own son. The arrogant Absalom was wily enough to understand the enormous influence Joab held over the king. Somehow he could sense that the fierce military man, either through outright bullying, or else by blackmail, could compel the king to comply with his wishes.

So Joab alone could arrange a meeting with David.

But Joab refused to come! He had lost interest in the vain young prince who now stood in total eclipse.

Angered by Joab's intransigence, Absalom in a fit of fury ordered his servants to set fire to Joab's barley crop that grew next to his own fields. The man must have had great charisma to get his servants to carry out such outrageous acts. They had murdered Amnon under his orders, and now they destroyed Joab's crop of grain.

Without further delay and in a towering rage, Joab

came to Absalom's royal quarters. *"Why did your servants burn up my barley?"* he stormed.

To which Absalom screamed back, *"And why did you bring me back from Geshur? I was better off there! If I have committed a crime let the king kill me for it! At least let me see my father's face!"*

Joab was astute enough to see he had no choice but to act. Now he had been trapped by the infuriated prince. There was no alternative; he would arrange an interview with the king. Father and son must meet. There had to be some sort of restoration. Surely it was not impossible to expect a reconciliation.

On the surface it might appear that Joab was a peacemaker. In reality it was not that at all. He was too tough, too cunning, too much of an opportunist to be that magnanimous. Instead he was acting again only in his own self-interest, hoping to curry the favor of both men, one of whom was bound to be monarch in the kingdom. And his own future depended on standing in royal favor.

Almost at once Joab arranged for David to see Absalom. The surly young prince prostrated his body before his father. Outwardly it was a symbolic act of homage. Yet within his will he still stood defiant, despising his father with a cruel and unyielding contempt.

David drew the prince to him, then kissed him.

It was the kiss of death.

For it was not true forgiveness. Nor was it a pardon!

There is such a thing as false forgiveness! It actually nourishes the seeds of crimes committed. It fosters their future growth. It only adds to the evil already perpetrated by the offender.

Neither David, Absalom, nor Joab could dream on this day what dreadful consequences would arise out of this false action. One cannot play games either with God or men in which we pretend to extend pardon to another while still holding them accountable for their wrongs.

Fortunately for us mortals, our Father above never does this. He forgives us completely through His own grace and generosity. Then, having forgiven us, He forgets all our failures against Him. Bless His name! (See Hebrews 10:15–24.)

13
Absalom Revolts Against David

David's failure to execute proper justice on his son served as a signal to Absalom that he could carry his sinister scheme for open revolt a step further without stern reprisals. His first move was to equip himself with a retinue of magnificent horses and chariots, along with a spectacular contingent of fifty footmen to run before him in pomp and ceremony, wherever he passed.

The use of horses and chariots had always been forbidden to Israel by Jehovah God. The reason was simple. The acquisition of superb horses meant they would have to return to Egypt for the best bloodlines. The training of fine charioteers, too, would entail depending on pagan people with ancient skills in this type of warfare. God would have no part of it. His people were to rely on His power to win their wars.

In one of his most poignant psalms, David makes reference to this truth: *"Some trust in chariots, and some in horses: but we will remember the name of the LORD our God"* (Psalm 20:7).

Absalom, however, flew in the face of God's wishes

and did precisely as he pleased to impress the people with his grandeur. He would play to his audience with a compelling performance.

His next cunning move was to curry the favor of all those who came to the capital, seeking justice and retribution for wrongs they suffered in the kingdom. In pomp and splendor the handsome prince sat at the gate of Jerusalem, acting as a self-appointed mediator to all who came with complaints.

Drawing the strangers to himself he would flatter them with a kiss, greet them warmly, then listen to their grievances. It was a sure way to win their loyalty and focus public attention on his own charms. *"Oh, if only I were appointed judge in Israel,"* he would sigh to them cunningly. *"All would be well in Israel."*

In part what he said was so, simply because at this point David had serious lapses in administering justice, even in his own family. In this insidious way Absalom, over a span of two years, actually succeeded in stealing the hearts and affections of the masses—this in spite of the fact that his father had been a national hero, an empire builder and a monarch dearly beloved in the realm.

Finally the fatal day came when the proud prince decided he could make his move to usurp the throne. For four years, since his return from Geshur, he had waited and worked for this moment. It was exactly forty years, too, since Samuel the ancient seer had anointed David at Bethlehem to be both shepherd and king over God's people.

Absalom advised David that he had made a vow to God, while still an exile in Geshur, that if ever he returned to Jerusalem, he would serve Him all his days. He now desired to go to Hebron, so sacred in Israel's tradition, and there perform his spiritual rites. As this spot was so sacred to David who began his rule over Judah there, it would also be special for him.

Again David was duped by his son's apparent spiritual impulses. Instead of being on guard, the king gladly bade him go in peace. Little did he even dream of the dire consequences both for himself and the entire nation.

Absalom had, by a carefully prepared underground network of intrigue, alerted his newly won followers all across the nation that when the bugles were blown in Hebron, he would be hailed as Israel's new monarch. In addition he had gathered around him a substantial band of men who gave him their loyalty, though being ignorant of his true intentions.

Last, but not least, the would-be king had prevailed upon Ahithophel, one of his father's most respected counselors, to come along and join him as a leading adviser. Perhaps the old man was flattered by the young man's offer of power.

Like so many revolts, the sudden emergence of a rival leader in the realm immediately polarized people. And the burning, frightening news came to David that most of Israel had turned against him. It appeared the general populace was gravitating toward the young impostor who was usurping power. At first David may have assumed it was a renewal of the old cleavage between Israel and Judah. He may have felt Absalom was exploiting the old animosities to divide the nation and bring about his downfall.

Besides the political and social implications of the sudden insurrection there was one thing which terrified David. He knew full well that his son was a ruthless, violent man. He was sure Absalom would not hesitate to assassinate both him and all his royal household to gain the crown. He was aware of the old grudges, the deep disdain and the corroding contempt that stained the young man's soul. It was this inner hatred that could drive the prince to commit the most atrocious crimes.

So in fear David decided to flee the capital!

It seems so out of character for one so courageous!

He who had always been so brave in battle, so heroic in the hour of crisis, so bold to face any foe, turned now to run in terror.

The issue was not one of arms and war. It was not a matter of mustering men for battle. It was not a case of physical combat to achieve military supremacy or political power. The issue here for David was much more profound. He faced a crucial spiritual contest within the sanctuary of his own spirit. Would he capitulate to God and allow Him to resolve this revolution in the realm, or would he, David, "the slayer of ten thousand," take matters into his own hands?

To his enduring credit, it must be said of David that above all else in life, he sincerely desired to do God's will. This was the vein of pure gold in his conglomerate character.

It did not matter to him how great the personal cost, how crushing the humiliation, how despicable the degradation he must endure as a man, he would pay any price to put things right between himself and the Most High. Nothing in all the earth mattered to David as much as honoring God and allowing Him to be preeminent in his affairs.

Here he stood now at the very lowest level of his entire career as a ruler in Israel. His own son had usurped the throne. His own people, whom he had served so well, had turned from him. His own military prowess had been eclipsed so that he was forced to flee as a fugitive from the violence of his own family.

It was an hour of darkness and horror and despair!

Exactly as Nathan had foretold, David faced the sword in his own family and bloodshed from his own offspring.

Yet David was sensitive enough in spirit, mature enough in mind, sturdy enough in soul to realize that all of this was a part of God's divine discipline for him. He saw clearly his own wrongs and was bowed humbly before his Father in heaven who now chastened him in compassion. He knew acutely that whom the Lord loves He corrects, in order to conform him to His own character (read carefully Hebrews 12:3–14).

Clearly, without any doubt, David's conscience was acutely aware that he had sinned against God—not only in his affair with Bath-sheba and his murder of Uriah, but also more recently in his failure to administer justice either to his own family or to the nation under him. So from this spiritual perspective he was a man contrite in spirit, humbled in heart, and utterly subdued in soul.

He gave orders for the entire royal household to be evacuated from the royal palace in the royal city. Ten concubines would be left behind to tend the house. He was to be accompanied by his royal bodyguard of six hundred fierce warriors drawn from the Philistines. He would have crowds following him who were still loyal to their beloved king as well.

Prominent among these was one of his favorite men of war—Ittai the Gittite. Though David tried to dissuade the dear fellow from coming with him, the pagan officer was determined to be with the king—whether in life or in death. Ittai would be loyal at any cost! It touched David deeply and little did either of them know at this low point in time, that down the road a short time later, when David returned to power, Ittai would be given the great honor to command one third of Israel's illustrious army.

Honor begets honor. Nor was David one to forget the devotion and friendship of those who stood with him in adversity. This dark and desperate hour would in time produce peace and power for both men under the providential hand of the Almighty.

Two others who wished to accompany David were his two faithful high priests, Zadok and Abiathar. Their desire was to have the Levites bear the Ark of the Lord out of the city to be with David, no matter where his exile and banishment might take him.

David disagreed with this idea. Somehow he seemed to feel that if the presence and power of the Most High remained evident in the tabernacle in the royal city, it could very well counteract any wickedness Absalom might devise there. Also he no doubt thought it would be a reproach on the honor and glory of God to have Him abdicate His place of honor in the capital city of Jerusalem. It was bad enough for David to relinquish his throne. But this must never, ever happen to the Most High.

In addition to all this, David was astute enough to see that Zadok and Abiathar, while still serving as priests, could also act as his underground agents and informers. Any news of developments in the city could be conveyed to him by their swift-footed sons, Ahimaaz and Jonathan.

These two young runners could act as couriers who would bring David all the latest news about Absalom, his army, his campaign plans and his new regime in the city. It was a clever arrangement.

David then left Jerusalem. He went on foot, barefooted. He no longer wore the royal crown on his head. His head was covered, probably sprinkled with dust and ashes to publicly declare his mourning—mourning for the loss of his kingdom—but more importantly, mourning for his wrongs against Jehovah God. And as he walked he wept. His wailing was not subdued or solitary. His weeping was open to the view of all his people.

The king was not indulging in self-pity! This was not a pathetic display of sorrow to elicit the sympathy of his followers, who had also joined him in covering their heads and weeping aloud. It was not even public mourning for a dying monarchy.

What David was demonstrating here was profound remorse for his own wrongs against the love and compassion of his Lord God. He, better than anyone else, recognized the great evil he as a man had perpetrated in Israel. Without apology or self-excuse he saw he had been deposed because what he had done displeased the Most High. In openness he was admitting his failures and acknowledging his wrongs. As king over a mighty empire he had despised his God and grieved His Spirit. Now in genuine remorse of soul and contrition of spirit, he repented openly before both God and men.

It was the sure and only path to peace with God.

It was the road to restoration and reconciliation.

It was the way to total healing and complete acceptance.

In his very own words David had stated the case clearly:

"If I shall find favor in the eyes of the LORD,
He will bring me back again!
But if He say—'I have no delight in thee'—behold,
Here am I, let Him do to me as seemeth good unto Him."

Solemnly, slowly the royal procession crossed the brook Kidron. They mounted steadily up the slope of Mount Olivet. There, on that sacred site, so well known to all the world, David bowed himself before God in humble worship. He *acknowledged* the Lord was God. David *accepted* the anguish of this dreadful day. He quietly *approved* of the arrangements God had made of all his affairs.

It was the spiritual catalyst needed at this precise point in history—required to release all the power of God on his behalf. Pardon, acceptance, peace, healing and restoration were all under way in the wondrous means God has in dealing with men amid their despair.

Just then Hushai showed up. He was one of David's favorite friends, an esteemed and highly respected counselor at the royal court. He was beside himself with grief at the plight in which his monarch stood. He had torn his robe in remorse and flung dirt on his head in despair.

But it is often when things look darkest that our God draws closest. And in this case He had special plans for poor old Hushai. He would prove to be the kingpin in the puzzle of how to unlock the dilemma of Absalom's revolt and bring the whole insurrection to a sudden end.

With guidance from God, David ordered Hushai not to stay with him, but rather to return at once to Jerusalem. He would meet Absalom there just as he entered the royal city in great pomp and power. Hushai was to offer his valuable services to Absalom. He would act as his right-hand adviser. And, as he was sensitive to the guidance of God's Spirit, he could neutralize and undo all the evil counsel given to the new king by the wise and crafty Ahithophel.

As things turned out this was exactly what happened. And the end result was that the insurrection was crushed in a matter of days. David would be restored to power and the entire nation would be spared from an atrocious civil war.

In reflecting upon all of this we are made to realize

how crucial is the conduct of those in positions of power and leadership. David's profound repentance and spiritual renewal were what spared his own life and that of his family and friends. It restored his throne; it saved the nation and pleased God.

The modern Church prays much for revival and renewal.

If it is going to come it will not begin in the pews! It must start in the hearts of those in the pulpit, in places of power and prestige, who can set an example for us, the common people, to follow.

14

David's Strength in Adversity

As David and his retinue of followers crossed over the rocky hills of Olivet a most unusual incident occurred. He was met by Ziba, in company with some of his servants, driving a string of donkeys.

One needs to read this account in one of the other older translations of the Scriptures to gather its full impact. In passing it may be of interest to the reader to realize that in preparing my Bible studies, I read each passage carefully from at least nine different translations of the Old Testament, and twelve of the New Testament. This is essential to gain a precise, yet multifaceted, understanding of the section studied.

Ziba, it will be recalled, was the man with fifteen sons and twenty servants whom David had made manager over all the property belonging to Saul's estate. He was responsible for tending the flocks, tilling the fields and managing the affairs of Mephibosheth, the crippled young man who was the only surviving offspring of Jonathan's family. He had been brought to Jerusalem and given the special honor to dine at David's royal table as if he were one of the king's own sons.

It was mentioned in a previous chapter that Ziba was an opportunist. He had the peculiar capacity to exploit any situation in which others were suffering loss or hardship. Here, now, he suddenly appears on the scene when David is fleeing for his life. Ziba comes just at the opportune occasion when David is under enormous stress of mind and distress of spirit. Not that he can give any sort of spiritual support or uplift—he simply was not that sort of man. But he came bearing huge quantities of bread, fruit, raisins and even a cask of wine on a string of asses, driven by his servants.

When questioned by David as to why he came, the cunning fellow gave a most convincing reply. The donkeys were for the royal family to ride on. Why go barefooted? The bread and fruit were for the young people to relish in their flight from the capital. And the cask of wine was to refresh anyone who grew thirsty and weary in the wilderness.

It all sounded so very gracious and generous of Ziba!

What it meant really was that he was dead sure David would never be back. His rule was over and done! Now was the opportune moment to play on the king's good graces and get back all the estate taken from him when given to poor Mephibosheth.

David asked where Mephibosheth was. Ziba's reply was an insidious slander on the young man, as later events would show. He stated that he had purposely chosen to stay in Jerusalem when the king fled into exile. This was because he was sure that in Absalom's revolt the dynasty of Saul's family would be restored to power. So he would be the legitimate successor to the throne.

It was an absolute fabrication. But in his mental anguish

David did not seem able to ascertain whether the tale was true or not. On the surface, at least, it seemed like a cruel stab in the back for all the kind generosity he had shown Mephibosheth across the years.

It was bad enough to be betrayed by a cruel son. It was worse still to be betrayed by his dearest friend's crippled son. Especially in this crisis.

Too hastily and too off-handedly, David turned to Ziba and told him to personally lay claim to all of Mephibosheth's estate. If the young man was that ungrateful for the king's bounties, he deserved to be stripped.

Ziba's crafty scheme had worked out exactly as he had hoped. In a single cunning move he had been able to recoup all his losses suffered earlier under David's generosity to Jonathan's family.

He thanked the king profusely. Then he sped off in glee.

He was a survivor—but only for a short while!

David and his entourage were now headed down into the fierce heat of the Jordan valley. It was a bleak and barren landscape scorched by the burning heat of the mideast sun. Its merciless oppression exactly matched the grief of his spirit and the grim adversity of his abdication as king over Israel and Judah.

As if this were not sufficient ignominy for him to suffer, a ruthless accuser suddenly appeared on the rocky slopes above him. His name was Shimei. He really was a rabble rouser who found special satisfaction in stirring up strife and controversy whenever it might embarrass the king. He came from the same tribe as Saul, the tribe of Benjamin, with a deep and bitter grudge against David and his family.

Shimei's home community was Bahurim. It may well have been a place which David despised because it appeared no benefit could ever come out of it. But later it will be seen how God brought great, great good out of this apparently evil place.

Like Ziba, this rebel was sure David would never be back. He was completely convinced the monarch had passed his zenith. Now he was obsessed with the notion that he could heap endless abuse on the king without any fear of reprisals. After all, David was finished and fleeing into the desert to fade from public view.

With utter impunity and furious disdain Shimei strode along the rugged hillside above the king and hurled abuses down upon him. Shimei cursed and swore and shouted insult after insult upon David. At the same time he picked up stones, rocks and clods of earth to hurl at the monarch in utter contempt.

It was an appalling performance. One might conclude that the wretched fellow really was mentally deranged. For certainly no man in his right mind would do such a dangerous thing. Especially so when David was being accompanied by his personal bodyguard of at least six hundred fighting men.

"You are a bloody man!" Shimei shouted angrily. *"You are a son of Belial—one who leads God's people to follow false gods!"* His face was black with rage as he ranted on, *"You usurped the throne of Saul—now God has wreaked revenge on you through Absalom's revolt. You are getting what you deserve!"*

Of course these were false accusations. The simple truth was David had never led Israel astray to follow other false gods. Nor had he ever usurped Saul's throne. If anything, the opposite was true. David, all during Saul's reign, despite his terrible tyranny, had shown the utmost respect for the Lord's anointed. Often he had restrained his young lions from wreaking their bloody revenge on the pathetic monarch. And his undivided loyalty to God was common knowledge.

What David had done that was so evil, and knew it, was to marry the pagan princess Maacah from Geshur in Syria. It was she who bore him Absalom. And the king was now reaping the consequences of his folly. More than that, he had established an evil precedent in Israel, one which even his own famous son, Solomon, would follow. This would be his ultimate undoing and precipitate the eventual collapse of the empire David brought to such grandeur.

It may well have been that David was sufficiently sensitive in spirit to realize that this was the stern rebuke he was receiving for this aberration in his life. Nor was he so dull in the midst of his debacle as to miss the message brought to him from the Most High through the sharp tongue and barbed words of Shimei.

David restrained his bodyguard from taking sudden and drastic action against Shimei. Abishai, especially, his blood boiling because of the abuse heaped on the king, would have rushed the rebel and severed his head. In a single stroke of his sword he could have silenced the cruel taunts and outrageous insults spilling from the quivering, frothing lips of the blathering Shimei.

But the king would have none of it. *"Let him alone. Let him curse. The LORD has directed him to do this!"* For David's followers this may have been an absolute absurdity. But for David it was the bedrock of his faith in God.

Shimei simply would not relent! Again and again like a persistent yapping terrier he harangued the king. He ran erratically along the steep slopes hurling down clods of earth, hot stones and even hotter words.

Not only was David steadily descending into the stifling

heat of the Jordan Valley, he was steadily being driven down into a ditch of stern and awful spiritual adversity. He was probably at the very lowest point of his entire spiritual pilgrimage!

The one sure and unshakable assurance which remained at this stage in his excruciating experience is best stated in his own words. *"It may be the LORD will look on my affliction, and that the LORD will requite me good for his cursing this day!"*

The great and wondrous consequence of David's calm confidence in the living Lord was that in the midst of this adversity he found enormous strength, inspiration and intimacy with God. It was at this time in his troubled life that he was given the imperishable lines of Psalms 20, 23, and 42. Of these, Psalm 23 and Psalm 37 have become my special favorites. Out of all the poetry this gallant man ever composed amid adversity under the inspiration of God's gracious Spirit they stand supreme. They have encouraged and heartened uncounted millions upon millions of souls across thousands upon thousands of years.

What was the psalmist's great secret?

What was the basic bedrock of his belief?

What was the sure source of his strength amid such grief?

It is this: *"Nothing that happens to God's child, no matter how excruciating it may be, does so by chance. Every detail is arranged by the knowing hands and understanding wisdom of God our Father. It is planned in love for our own good and His great honor. So, all is well, as we walk with Him!"*

It is this quiet assurance, this calm confidence in the living God which can insure that any child of God can triumph amid tragedy.

136

We do not blame our troubles and trials on others around us. We do not blame them on Satan, as so many are taught to do. We do not blame them on the cruel circumstances of our little lives. Rather we see our sufferings from our Father's noble perspective. We realize that they are the stern stuff He allows to come into our experience to conform us into His own beautiful character.

So in due time David and those with him crossed the burning Jordan plain. They came to the gentle, still waters of the river that flowed softly between its bushy banks. There in the lovely shade of the spreading trees they refreshed themselves and found solace for their spirits.

Beyond the river the king would find encouragement and support from old friends who stood with him amid his suffering and sorrow. Meanwhile back in the Royal City, in the providential arrangements of God, His Spirit was at work behind the scenes bringing the counsel of cruel men to an early end.

As directed by David, his friend Hushai returned to the great city. There he met Absalom who had also returned with a huge following of people from Israel, loyal to his cause, eager to overthrow the old ruler. Among them was Ahithophel, so highly esteemed as a counselor to kings, now willing to lend his full support to the young impostor.

In a brave show of supposed support for Absalom, Hushai shouted aloud *"God save the king! God save the king!"* Absalom was somewhat skeptical of Hushai's adulation. After all it was well known he was one of his father's closest friends. So he questioned him closely: *"Why didn't you go with David?"*

With bold-faced audacity and convincing sincerity, Hushai assured Absalom that if indeed he was to be the new king in Israel, chosen of God, and appointed by all the people, then Hushai's personal responsibility was to serve him well. Just as he had served his father David in whole-hearted loyalty, so likewise he was prepared to stay on in the city and serve his son. Apparently this declaration satisfied the suspicious Absalom, because later on he would turn to Hushai for advice in a most crucial decision.

Meanwhile the ambitious Absalom, eager to establish and consolidate his grip on the kingdom, turned to Ahithophel for guidance. What was the next important step he should take to seize power and send a clear message to all of the nation that he had usurped the throne?

Ahithophel's answer may well astonish and shock most of us. But a clear understanding of the primitive culture and crude customs of that era in human history will help us to grasp the full impact of the aged counselor's advice. Put very plainly, the crafty old man instructed Absalom to possess the king's harem, or at least as much of it as remained in the royal palace. It will be remembered that when David fled the city in such great haste, he left behind ten of his concubines to care for the regal mansion.

In ancient times the ultimate evidence and sure proof that one monarch had succeeded another was to lay claim to all his wives and concubines. It meant the previous ruler had been clearly supplanted and his place taken by the other. But this was generally only done after conquest in battle and total victory over the vanquished.

Here it was assumed, rather naively, both by Absalom and Ahithophel, that simply because David abdicated the throne, or at least appeared to have done so, the war was won. They seemed to forget what a military genius and ferocious warrior David could be. He was not dead yet, by any means!

In haste and excitement a temporary, gaudy tent was

set up on the flat roof of the royal palace. Soft bridal beds with their luxurious coverings were arranged there in full view of the whole city. Here Absalom would lie with each of the young and beautiful girls who had been David's concubines. By copulating with them in public view, for all to see, Absalom was proclaiming himself monarch of all he surveyed. It was a brash and evil action that would bring a swift and terrible end to his life. For this was a great sin in Israel and throughout her entire history.

Yet it was a precise fulfillment of Nathan the prophet's dire prophecy. For on the very same spot, on the rooftop balcony from which David had first seen Bath-sheba and lusted for her secretly, this revolting act was now performed publicly. The wheel of evil events in the life of David had now turned full circle. They had come back into full view to put him under dire reproach.

Ahithophel, the aged counselor, had tasted full revenge for the insult heaped upon his granddaughter Bath-sheba. For him it seemed justice was done. He imagined he spoke for God and so did others who heard him.

15
Hushai's Counsel Saves David

Stimulated by the ready response of Absalom to his counsel concerning the concubines, the venerable old Ahithophel proceeded to give him further advice on how to capture David. It was one thing to seize the royal harem. It was quite another to take the king captive. In dealing with David they were not facing some degenerate, soft monarch who knew only the luxury and pomp of a royal court. They were up against a formidable man of war with a tremendous reputation for bravery in battle.

Still Ahithophel, goaded by his greed for personal glory in the new regime, urged Absalom to let him take over command of his troops. The crafty old counselor was confident that by making use of the elements of surprise and overwhelming force he could capture David before he and his entourage crossed the Jordan into the wild terrain to the east.

Ahithophel seemed sure that if he could be allowed to lead a picked force of about 12,000 men in a sudden and immediate attack on the king, he could be captured. The cunning old man was sure David would surrender simply because he was at such a low point in his life—distraught by his son's insurrection, dismayed by the false accusations of others, disgraced by the great evils perpetrated in public against him.

What Ahithophel had forgotten in his pride of the moment was that David had been pursued for years by Saul and Abner, with 3,000 picked men, and never captured. He was too skilled in using wild and rugged terrain to outwit his foes. Ahithophel had also forgotten how David, even in the midst of great peril and apparent defeat, had learned to rely on God as the source of his salvation. He knew how to encourage himself in the Most High.

Nonetheless, at the first, Ahithophel's advice seemed to appeal to Absalom and the people with him. In actual fact they all seemed ready to go along with his battle plans.

But something prompted Absalom to seek a second opinion. Somehow he was not satisfied with just one man's counsel. So he ordered that Hushai, David's loyal friend, now serving as a double agent against him, be brought in before him. Little did the arrogant Absalom realize that Hushai was in truth God's man of the hour who would prove to be his nemesis. At enormous personal risk this doughty individual dared to stand before the ruthless Absalom and give counsel contrary to that of Ahithophel.

It would be the direct, divine answer to David's earnest, single sentence prayer when he fled from Jerusalem, *"Oh, LORD, I pray thee, turn the counsel of Ahithophel into foolishness!"* (*2 Samuel 15:31*).

With dignity and skillful diplomacy Hushai immediately refuted Ahithophel's advice. He reminded Absalom of his father's formidable fighting prowess. Not only that, he warned him that David was not alone, but had in

141

his company a contingent of battle-hardened veterans all of whom had been through tough campaigns with David. All of them were now fully aroused, ready for war, as eager to join battle as an enraged she-bear robbed of her cubs.

If the army of Israel were to launch an immediate attack they would suffer heavy casualities from David's ferocious forces. News of the losses would sweep the country, dishearten Israel and lead to sure defeat. No, no, indeed, such tactics were useless against a fierce opponent like his father.

As an alternative Hushai offered another suggestion. It was, no doubt, designed carefully by the counsel of God who honored Hushai's courage, to appeal to the young man's personal vanity and insatiable pride. It would flatter his ego and appeal to his passion for power.

Hushai urged Absalom, now that he had usurped the throne, to muster all the fighting men of Israel for battle. At least a third of a million men would be called to arms. All of them should assemble at Jerusalem.

More than that, it would demonstrate conclusively to the entire nation that Absalom had taken complete control of the affairs of state. To prove that he was the king in power, he himself, Absalom the Great, would go into battle leading his huge army like a gallant general against his doddering father.

Of course, Absalom, with his incredible vanity, could readily picture himself at the head of such a mighty army. With his magnificent physique, his handsome appearance, his splendid head of hair shining in the sun, he would be every inch the royal potentate. What more did a man need to make himself monarch of the majestic empire his father had established in the Middle East?

Hushai, seeing the growing light of grandeur glowing

142

in Absalom's eyes, added fuel to the fire of the young upstart's ambitions. He and his huge forces would simply descend like an overnight dew that covers the country, to trap David. They would find him wherever he fled. And even if he took refuge in some fortress city it would be pulled down and reduced to rubble, so that neither he nor any of his men could escape.

Completely inflamed by Hushai's vivid portrayal, the young rebel and his elders fell for this counsel. Little did they know that it was the Lord God Himself who was persuading them to adopt tactics which would spell their own total destruction and defeat.

What they failed to see was that such a plan would give David and his men ample time to cross the Jordan and escape into the wild regions to the east. It would also provide him with plenty of opportunity to muster those who were loyal to him and plan a skillful counterattack against his foes. Lastly, it would be an interval during which David could compose his soul, seek God's guidance and strengthen his own spirit in the Lord. God, in turn, would vindicate David's trust in Him.

Several salient truths become clear to us from this incident. The first is that there are times when God's people should be brave enough to run great risks for His sake in public office. Amid all the power politics and insidious intrigue which are a part of government, there is an opportunity for bold men and women to work there for the Lord. Their lives, their skills, their counsel can be used for the ultimate purposes God has in mind when He raises one leader to authority and puts another down in demotion.

Hushai was one of these people. And because of his own personal loyalty to David, and his respect for the Most High, he was used to spare the king's life and change the whole course of Israel's stormy history.

The second profound spiritual truth that emerges here is the vulnerability of human pride. Arrogance has always led to man's downfall. Few people, even within the Christian community, realize that God actually sets Himself against the proud. They do not know that He resists the arrogant. The reason is simple. Self-assertion, self-fulfillment, self-realization, all of which the modern-day church encourages, is the very antithesis of God's own self-giving life.

So it is not surprising that an arrogant young man like Absalom should suddenly be brought to a tragic end by his own innate pride. Are we astonished and horrified when we see in the next chapter how soon he is cut down?

Seduced by Hushai's advice that pandered to his pride, Absalom was destined for sure destruction. Yet, would-be preachers in our pulpits, who really are predators in disguise, urge their gullible people to *"Love themselves"—"Esteem themselves"—"Fulfill themselves"* in order to succeed, in order to gain recognition in a self-centered society, in order to be accepted in a crude and crass culture which has repudiated Christ and His call to lose ourselves for His sake.

God does not call us to be great people. He challenges us to deny ourselves in following Him. Thus He proves in us that he who is least is greatest, simply because He who lives in us is a *Great God!*

Hushai immediately alerted Zadok and Abiathar the priests, of the counsel both he and Ahithophel had given Absalom. As had been prearranged, all of this "inside information" was passed on to the two young men Jonathan and Ahimaaz, sons of the priests who were to run with the news to David. He was to be urged to cross the Jordan as soon as possible and seek refuge in the wild tumbled terrain to the east.

On their way the two youths were spotted by a lad who suspected they might be undercover agents. Absalom was informed of this and an immediate search was made in the area outside the city where they had been seen.

Fortunately the two runners knew a friendly family in Bahurim, who were sympathetic to David and loyal to his throne. They promptly put the youths down their well, covered its mouth with a large sheet and spread grain over it to dry in the sun. When Absalom's agents came searching for the runners they never suspected where they were. Instead they were sent on a false scent in another direction across the Kidron.

When the danger was past the two lads came up out of the well and sped off across country to warn David. It was a remarkable deliverance for the monarch and his entourage, for that very same night all of them crossed the river in safety to find sanctuary on the far side.

It is significant that the despicable community of Bahurim from which Shimei had come should be the very same one which God would use in a special way to spare David's life. David, no doubt, was sure no good could ever come out of this spot, only evil. But the Lord knew otherwise.

Things in life are not always as they appear to us. Because of our limited human capacities we cannot completely comprehend the full potential of all our circumstances in life. Often it is in the darkest hour and most threatening events that our Father is nearest to us, ready to deliver.

Often I must remind myself of that obscure yet marvelous passage in Nahum 1:3, *"The LORD hath His way in the whirlwind and in the storm, and the clouds are the dust of his feet!"* We all have our Bahurims where things appear so oppressive, so hopeless, so discouraging. Yet, if we will fully trust Him, out of these trying, cloudy circumstances the living God can bring us great good and surprising benefits. David found this to be a fact at Bahurim. So can we. In the darkest storm, *He is here!*

Not only because of Bahurim was the king spared, but also the counsel of his adversary Ahithophel was nullified. For now that David had escaped across Jordan there was no chance of carrying out his strategy to capture the fleeing monarch.

Ahithophel was astute enough to see at once that the winds of change were blowing across Absalom's kingdom, such as it was. He realized now that he was being displaced by Hushai as counselor. He grasped quickly that the wind of God's Spirit which had prevailed to convince Absalom that he should muster the whole nation for war, had at the same time blown away the last vestige of hope that he would ever be consulted again. He'd had his little day in the sun, but now his whole career was eclipsed and forgotten in the shadows.

As one who had been esteemed he was now set on the shelf.

His dignity was destroyed. His self-worth was shattered. He was no longer needed. So he was totally devastated.

Without show, fanfare or public protest, the tragic old man mounted his tiny ass, rode off home in despair to put his affairs in order. His fierce pride could not endure his demotion. Without question he was sure now, with a profound intuition, that because his advice was spurned, David was sure to survive and return to rule in the realm.

There was absolutely no future for him. He was done! So he hanged himself! His voice was stilled forever. He was gone! And another of David's most formidable foes was removed from the scene.

As so often happens in the affairs of men, once the tide turns it comes flooding back with tremendous force to change the entire landscape of life. This was happening for David. Where before his prospects were bleak and barren, appearing as if his rule had come to an ignominious end, suddenly the sky began to brighten and help was forthcoming from surprising sources.

He moved his forces to Mahanaim, the former royal city once occupied by the remnants of Saul's shattered family. This was where the hapless Ishbosheth had ruled briefly for two years before being massacred in his own house. It was also the spot where the Angel of the Lord appeared to Jacob. But most important by far, just now, it was the headquarters of Barzillai the Gileadite, a magnificent desert chieftain who had a great affection for David and held him in the highest esteem as a noble warrior.

Barzillai prevailed on his associates in the city to provide David with everything needed to sustain him in exile. Household furnishings, beds, basins, even earthenware of all sorts were supplied as well as ample provisions of grain, beans, lentils and pulse. All of these food items were battle rations; besides these he supplied such delicacies as honey, butter, mutton, lamb and cheese for the king's table.

Things were looking up! The tide had turned! God had laid a banqueting table in the wilderness for His own. *"Weeping may endure for a night, but joy cometh in the morning!"* (Psalm 30:5). David would never forget the occasion. On his deathbed he recalled Barzillai's kindness.

In the meantime Absalom began to prepare his battle

campaign to capture his own father. His first foolish move was to appoint Amasa, one of his own cousins, as commanding officer over all the forces of Israel.

Incongruous as it may seem, he was counting on this young warrior to overcome and defeat his own illustrious uncle.

His chances were slim indeed. He had no heart for it.

16

Absalom's Sudden Death

It was soon apparent that not all of the nation had turned away from David to follow his arrogant son. Thousands upon thousands of loyal fighting men quickly gravitated from all across the country to assemble at Mahanaim. This in itself must have been encouraging for David. He had fled from Jerusalem with only a small contingent of roughly six hundred picked men who were his personal royal bodyguard.

In the precious time bought for him by Hushai's counsel to Absalom, the battle-trained men loyal to David were formed into three fighting units. One was under Joab; the second was under Abishai his brave brother; and the third was under Ittai the Gittite, who was rewarded with this great honor for his devotion to David during his darkest hour.

The king himself saw to it how the contingents of fighting men were formed. He did not delegate this crucial responsibility to others. Moreover, he assured all of his comrades-in-arms that he himself would go into battle with them. This is most surprising! For it may very well have meant he could meet his own son in hand-to-hand combat. Nor was he any longer the ferocious young lion of former years. The passing seasons had taken their toll of his enormous energy and vigor. Still David was game to go with his men. His courage never waned!

His loyal troops, who were so fond of him, protested against this action. They insisted unitedly that he was worth at least ten thousand of his men. He was the prize piece in the war. The enemy forces in their drive to gain power would center their attacks on capturing him. If the king were taken, it did not matter how many men had to pay the supreme price with their own spilled blood.

No, no, he must not go into battle with them. As their beloved leader and supreme strategist, it was much better if he remained in command within the safety of Mahanaim.

David's response to such loyal devotion opens a window into his soul which is very revealing of the man's true character: *"What seems best to you, I will do!"* Obviously, in spite of his power and popularity with his people, David did not use his personal influence or charisma to override their wishes. He was at heart a truly "meek man." This does not imply that he was weak. Quite the opposite! He was a strong individual who could be appealed to and readily entreated by those under him. He was amenable to the advice of others, prepared to cooperate, if he felt their counsel was wiser than his.

David, as previous events have shown, certainly had some grievous weaknesses in his character. Yet his contemporaries still saw in him genuine greatness and this attribute of being approachable was one of his strengths— one of his sterling qualities as a leader.

The king had laid his battle plans with great care. Nor

was he about to sit quietly in Mahanaim and wait for Absalom to attack. His instincts told him to move quickly against the enemy. He would choose the ground and the time of combat. His forces would quickly cross the Jordan, traverse its hot plains, and climb into the rough wooded hills of Ephraim just north of Jerusalem. It would be an immediate threat to Absalom and draw him into battle on rough terrain where he could not use horses or chariots or cavalry units.

As the commanding officers and their fierce units filed out of the city, David stood on ceremony at the gate saluting each in turn. Above the muffled sound of their tramping feet he shouted encouragement to each unit, then added emphatically for all to hear, *"Deal gently with the young man, Absalom, for my sake!"*

David's brilliant tactics worked to perfection in the field. As soon as his men were within striking distance of Jerusalem, Absalom and his forces moved out of the royal city to engage the attackers. David's warriors were carefully positioned in the heavy, forested terrain. There were ambushes on every side. So a terrible toll was taken. In the first day of battle twenty thousand casualties were suffered. It was a horrendous loss equal to some of the greatest battles in World War II!

Absalom himself, so cocky, so proud, so self-confident, had ridden into the battle with his forces. He was astride a handsome mule, emblematic of royalty. He was so naive as not even to wear a helmet. Perhaps he felt his flowing head of long dark hair would be a symbol of prowess in combat. Vain fellow that he was, he had never spent a single day of his soft, luxurious life in combat. What did he know about war? He despised even the use of armor or a coat of iron chain mail to protect his chest. He must have assumed in his arrogance, like other leaders have, that he was invincible in battle, immortal as a god.

He was soon to learn a terrible lesson!

Coming face to face with some of David's ferocious men in the forest, he was startled by the sudden encounter. So was his stubborn mule. The frightened animal took the bit in his mouth and bolted for safety. Absalom could not control his mount. It rushed off through a tangle of trees, brushing its rider through the overhead branches and boughs. Absalom's long locks became entangled in the limbs of a tough old oak. He was dragged from the saddle to be left suspended in midair. The mule, blind with fear, rushed off on its own.

Absalom must not have even carried a sword or dagger. For, if he had, he could have easily cut himself loose from the tree. A single sweep of a sharp sword would sever his hair and set him free to flee. Instead he hung there helpless, fighting the limbs bare-handed.

A young warrior from Joab's contingent saw Absalom's plight. He remembered clearly what David had said as he strode out of Mahanaim. *"Deal gently with Absalom for my sake!"* What was he to do? In confusion of mind, he rushed off to find his commanding officer.

Joab's immediate response was, "Did you kill him on the spot? If so, I would gladly have rewarded you with a handsome bounty of silver and a beautiful robe!"

"Oh, no!" the flushed fellow replied, all embarrassed. "I could not raise a weapon against the king's son, especially since he entreated all of us to spare him!" His eyes glowed with devotion to David. "Even if you offered me a hundred times as much reward, I would not stretch out my hand to slay this royal prince!"

In an outburst of rage Joab refused to stand and debate the issue with the young warrior. He rushed up to where

Absalom dangled in the oak, thrashing about, trying to tear himself loose from its tough limbs. With sure skill and unerring aim Joab hurled three darts through Absalom's heaving heart. Blood spurted from the punctured chest wall. A few moments later he was cut down from the tree and put to death by several other warriors who accompanied Joab.

It was a drastic action demanded by drastic events.

Joab was not just avenging himself on Absalom for burning up his barley fields. He was not just settling an old score of revenge. Joab saw this as a sure shortcut to spare the nation from a protracted bloody civil war that could cost innumerable lives.

Joab was a hard-boiled, tough military commander who respected neither God, king, prince or any other person on earth. He was brutal beyond words to describe.

In utter contempt he flung Absalom's corpse into a hole in the forest. A huge pile of rocks was heaped over it in disgust. If Absalom wanted some sort of memorial to his wretched name, the pillar he himself had erected in pride would serve the purpose.

Without waiting for orders from his king, Joab on his own initiative had the battle bugles blown to announce the end of the conflict. Absalom's forces, mutilated and beaten, fled in disarray. The war was over! The enemies of David had been routed in total defeat. It was a brilliant though bloody victory! For the second time Israel was spared from a civil war which could have spelled national genocide.

All of this may have seemed somewhat glorious.

But the brilliance of the battle was marred by Absalom's grisly death. Its grievous impact on David would dull and tarnish the triumph of the hour.

How would he take the mixed news?

Even the redoubtable Joab seemed a bit troubled by this!

He knew so well the highly charged, emotional attachment which the king held for his wayward son. David's poetic nature and artistic temperament were easily aroused and readily torn by the trauma he endured because of this strong-willed young man who brought him so much grief.

Joab almost hesitated to send back the tragic word of Absalom's demise. Even if it could be somewhat tempered by the news of the peace that now prevailed in Israel, David, with his self-preoccupation with his son would not, could not, put things in proper perspective. Like so many indulgent parents he had narrow "tunnel vision" when it came to his children.

Ahimaaz, the notorious fleet-footed youth who could run like a gazelle, begged Joab for the honor of carrying the great news of victory back to David. After all it was he who had sped from Bahurim to the Jordan river to warn David to cross the stream ahead of Absalom's forces. He was keen to be of signal service again. But Joab was reluctant to let him run. Somehow in a subtle way the crafty commander seemed to feel that if the news were delayed a little, time would tend to take care of things a bit; delay was better than an immediate announcement.

There is no question at all that Joab was troubled by the ruthless action he himself had taken in killing Absalom. He saw it as his line of duty in combat. He felt he had saved the nation. But he also knew his deliberate disobedience of David's explicit commands to deal gently with his son would ignite a terrible outburst of grief in the monarch.

He had seen David's sorrow when the Amalekite brought news to him that he had slain Saul on the battle-field of Mount Gilboa. In that tragic hour he had his warriors kill the hapless Amalekite, even though he brought news of his ancient enemy's death. The king might well have the same sort of reaction again. If he did not demand Joab's death as full penalty for destroying his son, he might at least order the death of anyone who brought the evil news.

As a compromise measure Joab decided to send one of his retainers, a black servant from the region of Cush, now known as Ethiopia and the Sudan. He obviously considered this poor fellow expendable. If in his state of extreme agitation David decided to destroy him, it would not be as serious a loss as if he would kill a splendid youth like Ahimaaz.

It was a cruel choice. But Joab was not a man given to great tenderness at any time. The black slave would be a small price to pay to preserve his own life. So Joab sent him off with the deadly news. He was ordered to tell the king all that he had seen.

Meanwhile Ahimaaz continued to press his commander to let him run to David. Joab kept stalling, but at last relented when he felt confident Cushi would be there before him. In eager exhilaration Ahimaaz sped off across the plain, took a shortcut across the Jordan, and came within sight of Mahanaim first.

David was sitting in state at the city gate when suddenly the lookout in the tower above him called down that he could see a lone runner coming. His fluid motion, so smooth, so fleet of foot, made him sure it was Ahimaaz.

David was delighted! He was so fond of young Ahimaaz. He was a fine lad who was bound to be bringing good news. But the watchman in the tower saw a second runner behind him now approaching. His pace was slower and a little more ponderous.

At first all Ahimaaz could call out to the king as he collapsed at his feet was, *"All is well!"* It was really only a half-truth. When he got his breath and was questioned more closely he reported that all he knew was the enemy had been defeated amid a great tumult of confusion.

By this time the black runner arrived. Shining beads of sweat glistened silver against his dark skin. He, too, was a beautiful man. But he bore deadly, devastating news. In his blunt, honest, open manner he did not try to parry David's question, *"Is Absalom safe?"* All he blurted out was, *"The enemies of my king, and all that rise in revolt against you are dead!"*

Each word struck the king with terrible impact. It was as if the cruel darts Joab had plunged into Absalom's chest had in fact been driven into David's heart. He was utterly convulsed by the news. The dreadful message devastated him.

Turning away, alone, he climbed the dark stairs to a small chamber over the gate. And as he went he cried, *"O my son Absalom, my son, my son, Absalom! Would God I had died for thee, O Absalom, my son, my son!"*

In his agony and anguish, in his outpouring of sorrow, David seemed oblivious to the grief of others. At least twenty thousand other families had lost either a son, a father or a brother in that day's battle. But he seemed to care little! All he could see was his own loss. Yet the whole nation was spared in its darkest hour!

17

David Returns as King to Jerusalem

In his highly charged emotional convulsion David refused to be comforted or consoled. Nothing anyone could say or do seemed to be of any avail whatsoever. It was as if the darkness of night had descended upon his spirit and even the last stray star of hope had been quenched in his sensitive soul.

It is possible that a great part of his pain was a poignant regret for his own failure as a father to discipline and correct his children under God. David may well have realized by this time that the wickedness and waywardness of both Amnon his firstborn son and now Absalom his third son were a reflection of his own unwillingness to admonish them in the things of God. Nor had he set before them that exemplary example of a truly noble life which might have induced them to follow in his footsteps.

Whatever all the reasons may have been, the king grieved so deeply that day, his gloom cast a grim shadow over all around him. In the usual manner of human affairs word sped swiftly across the grapevine of gossip that David behaved as though the death of his son was of much greater consequence than the remarkable victory won for him by his valiant fighting forces.

Or, to put it another way, his personal, parental grief had so warped his perspective that it seemed not to matter to him one iota that twenty thousand other gallant men had lost their lives in the struggle. His view was so selfish, so narrow, so distorted that it brought shame on those who had fought so bravely to save his throne, rescue his family and preserve his empire from total anarchy.

When word of this reached the crusty field commander, Joab, he went roaring back to Mahanaim in a rage. He was not one to take such absurd behavior with calm objectivity. Joab was not a diplomat. He was a tough soldier!

Without any apologies for his own violent part in the death of Absalom, Joab stormed into the king's presence. His eyes flashing with hostility, his teeth clenched in anger, his jaw muscles taut as steel cables, he launched into a terrible, yet valid, tirade against David.

"You have disgraced and shamed all the warriors who risked their lives for you! We saved you, your wives, your family and your people! You act as if you love your enemies and hate your friends! So much so you give the impression it would have pleased you if we had all perished and your 'no-good son' had survived!"

David was silent, stunned by this shock treatment.

Joab was telling the truth.

It brought the king back to reality.

The commanding officer stormed on in unbridled anger: "Get out of this cozy chamber! Get out of your self-pity! Get out of your self-centered grief! Get out among your men and share some of their sufferings! Get out to the gate of the city and give encouragement and cheer

158

to those coming back after such a victory!"

His advice, crude as it might seem, was the best therapy in all the world.

"If you don't," Joab's voice rumbled ominously, like a volcano about to erupt, "all your people will desert you. You will be abandoned, left utterly alone. Then your end will be worse than any terror you suffered up until now!"

David was humbled, mortified, but also aroused.

He would arise and go out to the gate to greet the victors.

The nation would know again he was truly their monarch.

The principle here is a most crucial one. As Christians we dare not allow our personal sorrows over our own families to so convulse us that we are no longer of use to God or others. We must not cast gloom and doom on others around us simply because we are in grief. Rather, as we move out to touch others and share in their suffering, our own burdens will be lightened and lifted from us.

For David, this point in history was a crucial juncture. He actually stood in great jeopardy, and so did the entire nation of Israel. If the people perceived that he had lost the capacity to lead them with courage, and command them with strength, they would fragment.

What both Israel and Judah needed desperately again was the reassurance that David was indeed a great enough monarch to reunite them under his authority.

Most of the common people apparently had little if any understanding of the intense inner, spiritual struggles which convulsed the king's soul. Even among the elder statesmen only a few ever grasped David's true genius under God. All they wanted was a strong man who could lead them to power. Like most nations they craved a national hero around whom they could rally.

David had appeared to be such before the insurrection of his son Absalom. But when he abdicated the throne so easily, many wondered where they stood. Now again it was time to see if David was great enough to gather the diverse sections of the state into a single unit again. Did he still have the courage and charisma to consolidate the people?

Strange as it seems, the tribes of Israel, now in disarray and defeat, were the first to send him word they would like to have him back in Jerusalem as their monarch. It must have been great good news for the distraught king, perhaps the most cheering prospect he had seen in a long time.

What puzzled David, still ensconsed in Mahanaim, was the strange reluctance of the men of Judah to welcome him back. He decided on a clever diplomatic move to win their support. First he would let them know of Israel's advances, then he would remind them of his family ties to them. Lastly he offered Amasa the honor to become his commander-in-chief in place of Joab whom he was determined to demote.

To the very end of his life, David had trouble handling Joab and his younger brother Abishai. One wonders why he did not simply dismiss both of them from his service. Yet the irony was he seemed to need their ruthless courage and rough loyalty to complement his own more gracious character. But now that Joab had killed Absalom, David felt more deeply wronged by his tough commander than ever before. Amasa simply must replace him, even though it was Absalom who had chosen Amasa to fight against his own father. How complex and convoluted human behavior can be!

These were complicated times amid the chaos of the

short-lived civil war that had come crashing to such an early end. In part its brevity was because of Joab's boldness. Now David had to pick up the pieces and put the nation together again. Plans were made hastily to bring him back to the royal city. Even in this triumphant return there would be bickering and rivalry between Judah and Israel. Like so many spoiled children, these factions never seemed to mature into a noble nation.

An elaborate ferry was provided to take the royal family back across the Jordan. They would not wade across in fear as they had when they fled. And wonder of wonders, the first party to meet them on the other side was none other than Shimei, the horrible accuser, accompanied by about a thousand of his cronies from around Bahurim.

In terror for his very life he prostrated himself in the hot sand on the river bank at David's feet. Openly he admitted his great wrongs against the king. Earnestly he apologized for his perverseness in hurling insults and stones and clods of clay at David. Sincerely he confessed his sins and cast himself on the monarch's mercy.

Abishai wanted no part of it. "Off with his head!"

But David was much more generous. For a second time he spared the scoundrel's life! A second time he forgave his faults! A second time he extended compassion!

Yet, like most human beings, he never forgot Shimei's insults.

Even on his deathbed, in the last instructions given to Solomon who would succeed him, David made sure Shimei would be dealt with in severity.

Therein lies the great difference between our human forgiveness and our Father's forgiveness. We cannot seem to forget completely the wrongs others have done to us, whereas God has the gracious capacity for forgetting our iniquities and not remembering them against us again

(Hebrews 10:17). Bless His dear, dear name!

Though Shimei was the first to meet David from all of Israel, he was not alone. With him came the foxy Ziba, along with his fifteen sons and twenty servants. Like Shimei he never dreamed David would be back. Both men knew full well that unless they made skillful moves to curry the king's favor, their days were over when David was reinstated in power on the throne.

Mephibosheth also came. He was a pathetic picture! He resembled a ragged scarecrow. Since the day, the awful day, that David fled the Royal City, barefoot and weeping, Mephibosheth had lived in despair. He had neither trimmed his toenails nor washed his crippled feet. His ragged beard, stained and tangled, hung in long wisps around his unshaven face. His clothes were filthy, wrinkled and unwashed, reeking of filth and perspiration.

He was a repulsive sight. He appeared like a leper or destitute beggar from the bazaar. Certainly he was not fit to meet the king. But he came to cast himself upon the mercy of the returning monarch.

David did not seem to be overly impressed with the young man's appeal. He questioned him closely as to why he had not come with him when he left Jerusalem. In the back of his mind the king may have felt Mephibosheth was masquerading. Somehow he did not trust him fully.

Mephibosheth insisted Ziba had slandered him when he reported to David that he still had designs on the throne. He claimed he had asked for an ass on which to accompany the king when he fled, because he was a cripple. But Ziba had deliberately denied him this request. So what could he do?

In any case the poor fellow was so pleased the king was coming back now. He esteemed David as highly as an angel of mercy. He was bound to do what was best.

It was he who had shown such incredible generosity to him before. Now again he could be counted on to be gracious.

It was a touching tribute. It might have moved some men profoundly. But David simply was not much impressed. Perhaps he was weary of all the knavery and duplicity which swirled around him in the chaotic time of confusion. He was fed up with being double-crossed and betrayed by those he trusted. So he was in no mood to try and adjudicate complex quarrels between cunning conspirators.

Almost in a huff he cut short Mephibosheth's pleas.

He did not want to hear more about his quarrels.

He and Ziba were to divide Saul's estate.

The decision did not seem to deter Mephibosheth. Quite the opposite. He was ecstatic the king had come back. He was not only his benefactor but also his hero. Even if Ziba swindled him out of all he had, *all was well!* Long live the king in peace and security.

In vivid contrast with Shimei, Ziba and Mephibosheth was the loyal and trustworthy old Barzillai. He had stood as a tower of strength to David during this ordeal. When so many had devious designs against David in his time of trouble Barzillai provided him with shelter in his city, equipment for his family and huge quantities of food supplies for his forces. The venerable old gentleman accompanied David down to the Jordan to bid him farewell.

The king entreated Barzillai to accompany him all the way back to Jerusalem. He offered to treat the eighty-year-old veteran with the honor and esteem of a father. He could live in royal quarters and dine at David's table in dignity.

But the white-haired desert chieftain declined this generous offer. He insisted he was past the age when royal

163

delicacies and regal entertainment held any appeal for him. He preferred to live out his life in the simplicity of his old familiar haunts. He wished to die and be buried with his forebears.

Still he deeply appreciated David's great generosity. In his place Chimham his son could go and live with the king as a royal prince. He could receive the same noble treatment that David had bestowed on Mephibosheth. So the king agreed and took the young man with him. He kissed the aged chief a fond farewell after blessing him.

In the midst of all these personal encounters, perhaps unknown to David, there rumbled throughout the country endless controversy between Judah and Israel as to who should accompany him back to Jerusalem. It was all so petty and so infantile it scarcely deserves our attention. The endless rivalry between these two factions reminds one of the pathetic political disputes that have ravaged Ireland for so long. Eventually, they would tear Israel in two. Only David's greatness could overcome the differences, the divisions and the cruel suspicions.

God's people need to be reminded that disputes and quarrels which lead to evil divisions are regarded by *Him* to be just as wicked as adultery, drunkenness or witchcraft (read carefully Galatians 5:13–21). He has given to us His gracious Spirit of unity and harmony. Why then do so many indulge in strife and discord? There can be no blessing, no peace, no rest, no strength that way!

This was a profound principle the people of Israel were slow to learn—even in David's day and under the genius of his government.

18

The Deaths of Amasa and Sheba

Before David had been escorted in state back to the seat of power in Jerusalem, the antagonism between the men of Israel and those of Judah flared into an angry confrontation. Accusations and counter-accusations were hurled at one another. Jealousy, envy and heated animosity arose from the banked fires of old rivalries.

Israel insisted that her ten tribes had a much larger share in the national scene than did Judah. So theirs was the right to have a prior place in the royal palace. Judah on the other side insisted that David was one of her native sons, bone of her bone, flesh of her flesh, one on whom she had first claim.

So provincial and so petty were the hostilities they tend to weary one with their childish overtones. Yet, on the other hand, they comprised a constant hotbed of discontent in the nation which put the monarchy in great peril. It was the sort of situation that anyone jockeying for power could exploit for his own selfish ends.

There is nothing new about this in the long, tedious history of human affairs. Dispute is everywhere at work, both in politics and in private family disputes. It is rivalry, jealousy, envy and discontent which erupt to wreck the best-laid plans of man or church or state. Our part as God's people is to be peacemakers amid the mayhem. We are called to be loyal to the leaders whom God the Most High has set over us. We are expected to be faithful in the line of duty, diligent in bringing about unity and good will.

At this juncture in David's stormy reign there seemed to be a dearth of such devoted and loyal supporters on whom he could count with solid assurance. It was as if he was caught in the cross-currents of evil events over which he had little control. Ferocious fellows were conspiring against him and against one another to gain advantage. Some were rank opportunists who saw his precarious position as a chance to further their own ambitions.

One of these was Sheba, from the tribe of Benjamin. He evidently was a rather popular person with a large following still loyal to Saul's dynasty. His claim was that Israel really had no part in David. He was in fact a foreigner. Why should they follow him? Instead let their men each go his own way and somehow choose a new leader of their own. Nor was he slow to offer himself as the new national hero. Absalom was dead now. He himself could very well take the impostor's place.

Like so many stupid sheep that unwittingly submit to the mob instinct, the men of Israel rallied to his cause. It seemed they could be induced to do whatever he wished. All he needed to do was criss-cross the country to rally full national support.

By the time David returned to Jerusalem he faced another national emergency because of the notorious Sheba. Instead of coming back to power with joy and in peace, he was returning to rule this obdurate, stiff-necked race under a lowering cloud of intrigue and conspiracy. His double dilemma was that he could no longer call on the military might of Joab to head up his armed forces, since he had been demoted and broken in rank.

Almost in desperation David hastily summoned Amasa to come to his aid. He ordered the commander, who only a few days before had been his antagonist under Absalom, to muster the men of Judah again for war against Sheba. David was not about to abdicate the throne again. He would not leave the royal city. This time his forces would take the initiative and attack Sheba at once to destroy him.

It is not surprising Amasa could not rally the warriors of Judah as quickly as David wished. No doubt many of them considered him a turncoat who had gone over to Absalom's side and actually fought against them. Why should they come under his command? So time was running out for David and the king was uneasy when Amasa failed to muster his men.

In his insistence on an immediate attack against Sheba, David then turned to Abishai, Joab's gallant younger brother. He ordered him to take his most notorious fighters as well as his own royal bodyguard and pursue Sheba. Abishai was quick to respond, eager to go, ready for battle. He always was! He was a remarkable warrior of enormous loyalty to David.

The strange yet incredible thing was that joining him in battle was the irrepressible Joab. Though demoted by David and stripped of his rank, the crusty, tough commander came into the field under Abishai fully armed, sword in sheath, girded in mail, ready for battle. Difficult he could be, cruel as a tiger, ruthless in his behavior, Joab was still utterly loyal to David.

167

He and Abishai overtook Amasa at Gibeon, the special spot where roughly twenty years before David and his men heard the wind of God's Spirit moving through the mulberry trees. That had been a time of great victory over the Philistines. Now Joab hoped he could carry off a second conquest in the same place. This time it would not be over the enemy Philistines. It would be a personal triumph over his archrival, his own cousin Amasa, who had supplanted him as commander-in-chief.

He greeted Amasa with apparent great good cheer, *"How is your health—my brother?"* Joab exclaimed as the two embraced. Swift as a flash of light Joab seized Amasa's beard as if to kiss him; then in the same instant, he swept his short dagger from its sheath and plunged the razor sharp steel into his adversary's abdomen.

It was a mortal stroke. With a quick and furious turn of his wrist, Joab disemboweled the unarmed general. He collapsed in a heap, the blood rushing from his chest cavity. There he wallowed in it until a few moments later he was dead.

It was Joab's third deliberate murder. In cold blood he had killed Abner, Absalom and now Amasa.

The score was settled. He would allow no one to supplant him as David's foremost general. He had taken matters into his own blood-stained hands. And anyway, what could David say? Hadn't he arranged the brutal, heartless murder of Uriah? It was a dreadful deed with which he could blackmail the king to the end of his life. What was more, Amasa was not an innocent man, loyal to David, as Uriah had been. Amasa had been a traitor who turned against David and dared to confront his forces in battle. No, as far as Joab was concerned, justice had been done.

Briefly the bloody corpse lying on the road made the men following Abishai pause and hesitate to see who the casualty might be. Joab exploited the situation and ordered one of his men to alert everyone who came along to give Joab and David full allegiance. Amasa had been liquidated, the coast was clear, Joab was in charge again. On with the war!

Then Amasa's corpse, now covered with a swarm of flies, feeding on the blood and gore, was dragged off into the brush. A cloth was flung over it. There would be no further need for this grisly evidence of a change in command. The first man in the new conflict had fallen. Under Joab's brilliant yet brutal tactics he might just be the last in a war that had strange and terrifying turns to it.

Meanwhile back in the city of David, the returning king tried to restore some order in his own household as well as in the realm. In a thoughtless and harsh action he removed the ten concubines from the palace and put them into a private ward. Here they would be forced to live in abject widowhood for the rest of their tragic and tearful lives. Never again would they know the warmth of a man's affection or enjoy the rich fulfillment of bearing children whom they could cherish in their bosoms.

It was no fault of theirs that they were chosen to be David's concubines, as it was no fault of theirs that they had been left behind in Jerusalem. Or that they had been disgraced and raped in public by Absalom.

Such was the hard and terrible treatment of women in a crude culture and even more cruel society. Anthropologists and other would-be advocates of primitive peoples would have us believe that all was beautiful and pleasant in ancient societies. Not so! Women in particular were maltreated and abused in many ways. And David's harsh handling of these ten young concubines does him no credit at all. His decision to banish them stands as a dark blemish on his record. The only plausible reason was his personal desire to disengage himself from Absalom's atrocity.

Sometimes we of the West forget the great emancipating influence of the gospel on human society. Without it the world would be ten times harder than it is. And David did the Most High no great honor by his action here. It really was a disgrace! He could have shown them great compassion.

While David reestablished himself on the throne in the royal city, his field commanders Joab and Abishai pursued the elusive Sheba all across the country. Like a pair of hounds on the trail of a hare, they simply would not relent. Finally the cunning conspirator was brought to bay in a small town, well fortified, called Abel. It was a frontier fortress in the far northern reaches of Israel. This was an unusual community, famous in those days for the peculiar power of its people to give sound advice and wise counsel to anyone who was perplexed by insoluble problems. Like Naoth, where Samuel used to reside with his school for young prophets, it may have been a center which drew men and women of unique spiritual insight to it.

No doubt Sheba fled here not only to escape from David's resolute warriors but also to seek counsel for his next move against the king. But it was too late! He was overtaken in the city. The gates were slammed shut against Joab's fighting forces, and Sheba was penned inside like a rabbit in a box trap.

Joab was not about to be beaten by the little town of Abel. He was the invincible commander who in his stormy career had breached the defenses of such formidable fortified cities as Jerusalem and Rabbah. He would easily take Abel. So with grim determination he ordered his men to cast up a giant earthen bank against the outer walls. His fighters would simply storm the citadel without delay.

This may all seem rather matter-of-fact military strategy. But when we pause to remind ourselves that it was all being done by an officer who at this point did not even hold a commission from the king, it is a startling account. Joab, incorrigible general that he was, pressed the battle against Sheba with fury. Still loyal to his monarch, still devoted to his nation, he saw clearly that only Sheba's death could restore strength and unity to the kingdom. His own rank or position was not the main point, it was the greater good of his people. So even though Joab was brutal, there ran through his character this special quality of his utmost devotion to duty as he saw it.

As the earthworks gradually approached the top of the city wall, a woman came and stood upon the parapet and shouted down to the men to call Joab. She wished to counsel him. It is astonishing the tough, crusty commander would even comply. In those days women were considered of little account. Why should a battle-hardened general even listen to her chatter?

But the marvel is, he did!

Like Abigail who had appealed to David to spare her husband and family, so this wise woman appealed to Joab to spare her community, her people and her family from sure extinction. She entreated him to be merciful and not to sin against the Most High in destroying His own special people.

To his credit Joab was willing to give her a hearing. He did not just turn away from her petition.

Instead he struck a shrewd bargain with her. "Give

me Sheba and I will withdraw from the attack," he shouted back at her between cupped hands.

"His head will be tossed down to you over the wall," she screamed back in startling confidence and sure faith.

How she prevailed upon her people to behead the wily fellow we are not told. The grim deed was done in short order and the grisly, bloody skull was thrown over the wall to fall at Joab's feet. It was much better than if the city walls had fallen.

With his powerful fighting instincts, Joab knew that was all he needed to end the insurrection. Just as Absalom's sudden death ended the first, now Sheba's assassination ended the second assault on David's throne. He ordered the battle trumpets to be blown. The seige was over! The war was ended! Great loss of life had been averted by the wise woman's counsel. He and his rampaging warriors could return home in peace. For Joab his sudden victory was sufficient to reinstate him once again as David's commanding officer.

Perhaps, for a time at least, peace would prevail in Israel.

The king now felt constrained to make some major appointments in the kingdom which would assure greater stability in the matters of state.

He set Benaiah, one of his most gallant generals, over his personal bodyguard. In the course of time it would be Benaiah who would actually assassinate Joab. Besides him David appointed brilliant men to be his treasurer, his historian, his record keeper and his secretary—and other lesser administrators as his personal advisors.

Perhaps most important, he retained Zadok and Abiathar to be his high priests in the royal city. The time was at hand when he should give much greater attention to the spiritual welfare of his people.

19

The Drastic Death of Saul's Seven Sons

The first dramatic evidence that indicated a great need for spiritual renewal within Israel was the severe devastation of a three-year famine. Not that famines were uncommon in the Middle East. They were not, nor have they ever been. Even back to the ancient days of Abraham, Isaac and Jacob, periodic droughts ravaged Palestine and portions of North Africa.

The tribes and nations of this immense region have always had to fall back on the irrigated crops grown along the Nile River in Egypt to survive. Loss of livestock, decimation of crops and the pathetic plight of people facing starvation was part and parcel of the life in the area— exactly as we have seen in Africa in recent years.

However, it has always been clearly understood, even by pagan societies, that such famines were in fact more than mere natural phenomena. They were in part also a form of divine judgment and providential discipline upon those who disregarded God. This David knew without any doubt, just as Ahab would know in the days of Elijah when a similar famine came upon Israel.

173

Sincerely now the king sought spiritual counsel of the Most High through Zadok and Abiathar. If there was a specific sin in the nation that accounted for the calamity, he would take steps to correct matters. After all he was the spiritual shepherd of his people under God's great hand. He had this serious responsibility.

To his surprise it was disclosed clearly that the drought had come because of Saul's deliberate attempt to exterminate the Gibeonites. These were the offspring of a small clan of Canaanites who had come to Joshua in disguise four hundred years before and sued for peace after the capture of Jericho and Ai. Without consulting God, Joshua had formed a league with the Gibeonites. Later he was to discover that he had been deceived by their intrigue. But rather than break his oath of peace to them, he stood firm to his commitments not to harm them. But he bound them into servitude to Israel forever. They were to be hewers of wood and drawers of water destined to serve the Levities who cared for the Tabernacle and all the offerings of sacrifices in Israel.

Saul, in his apparent eagerness to impress his people, had simply ignored the sacred bond between the two races. In his folly he tried to exterminate this group, just as he had earlier assassinated the eighty-five priests of Israel at Nob in the days of Ahimelech. Now the nation was bearing the penalty for his wrongdoing.

In our permissive society the breaking of promises, the disregard of solemn vows, the failure to honor contracts are considered of little consequence, just as Saul did. But from God's perspective this is a most serious offense. As our Lord Himself reiterated again and again, *"Let your yes be yes and your no be no!"* We are to be judged in full measure by the verbal commitments we make to one another. A man's word should be his bond. This is required of those who call themselves God's people.

Sad to say, even few Christians can be counted on to do this, whether in business or in social relationships.

David, to make amends for this evil that had been perpetrated in Israel, conferred with the Gibeonites to see what compensation could be made. Their reply was astonishing! Far from being that of a purely mercenary settlement, which might be expected of a pagan Canaanite race, they requested a full spiritual atonement, based upon the divine Levitical law ordained by God Himself. This was clearly stated in Numbers 35:29–34. There the precise procedure of carrying out capital punishment was delineated to make appropriate recompense for the death of innocent victims.

What they demanded was not gold or silver, or even land, property or freedom from serfdom; rather it was the sacrifice of some of Saul's offspring to compensate and atone for those he had murdered. David clearly grasped the validity of their claim and set about at once to see it was carried out.

There are many strident voices in the contemporary scene who protest that capital punishment is a grossly cruel, inhuman action unworthy of a civilized society. They claim it is a carryover from the "dark ages" and inappropriate to our so-called *enlightened age.*

Few understand the divine principles behind this form of justice. God, who is love, is unselfish. He is, rather, completely self-giving, self-sacrificing, self-sharing. Therefore, to Him it is the very antithesis of His life, His love and His character when one human in an act of utter selfishness and self-assertion murders another, thereby depriving the victim of life, God's greatest gift. Consequently the only appropriate penalty which the offender can pay is to forfeit his own life. The only adequate atonement is to answer the victim's agony and anguish with his own death.

This is not some sort of savage vengeance. It is a step ordained to protect human society from the violence of its own vicious members. Contrary to all that sociologists say, this form of justice does deter homicides. Yet, even in countries where the general populace ask that capital punishment be reinstated, obdurate governments refuse to do so. Then they wonder why their penal system is a laughingstock to criminals and their courts are despised. While all the time victims, and their families, suffer endless anguish without proper retribution or justice.

David was bold enough to take severe steps to see that the cruel deaths of innocent Gibeonites be paid for properly. He promptly selected seven offspring of Saul's family to be slain. Without question he was assisted in this by the high priests who made the final decision in such difficult matters. From our perspective this choice of a subsequent generation to atone for the crimes of their forefather seems grossly unfair. The only possible position one can accept is that it is one family unit paying in full for the wrongs committed against another family unit. Benjamin as a tribe versus Gibeon as a tribe! Blood for blood.

Of the seven young men chosen to pay the supreme price, two were born to Rizpah. She had been one of Saul's attractive young concubines. After his death it was claimed by Ishbosheth that she had an affair with Abner, Saul's commanding officer. This so enraged the general that he switched his allegiance to David, thus leading to the eventual unification of the entire nation under David's monarchy. Why her sons were chosen we shall never know.

The five other lads were young men born to Merab.

She was Saul's eldest daughter. In actual fact she rightly belonged to David. He had won her hand in battle by slaying Goliath. But Saul defrauded young David of his prize by giving the girl to Adriel instead. Adriel and Merab had five sons between them. Then Merab passed away.

Out of a sense of utter frustration, because of her own barrenness, Michal, David's wife, had taken over custody of these five boys and reared them for Adriel. It may have been a way for Michal to find some sort of feminine fulfillment since she had no children of her own. But for David the five boys must have been a constant reminder of Saul's utter contempt for him as a brilliant young warrior. So in part this choice may have been partly motivated by a desire for personal revenge on Saul's family, and also as an insult to Michal who had not only been disloyal to him, but who despised him in her heart of hearts.

If so, the action did him no great credit, but rather was a reproach upon his reputation. We cannot be sure!

The death of the seven young men in public view, all on the same day, was a monumental event in Israel. For the youths were not just hung by a noose as one might imagine. They were actually crucified in that most cruel and atrocious form of ancient torture devised in Mesopotamia, known and practiced long centuries before the advent of Christ. It was often referred to simply as "hanging on a tree."

Though this dreadful spectacle took place in April, about the time of barley harvest, Rizpah, mother of two of the young men, refused to be comforted or consoled for almost six months. In anguish of soul and agony of spirit she stood watch over the corpses of her crucified boys. Draped in sackcloth and using the same material spread over a huge rock, where the crosses stood, as her couch, she drove off the scavengers that came to feed on the decomposing carcasses. She screamed at the vultures, ravens and crows that came by day. She hurled rocks and stones at the jackals and hyenas that prowled around at night.

When word of her vigilance and unending sorrow came to David he was deeply touched. God's Spirit convicted him then that all his motives in this execution of judgment had not been pure or unselfish. He suddenly realized that in truth he had heaped excessive abuse on Saul's family. He himself would now have to make some sort of royal retribution to the offended family.

To his credit he immediately ordered that the bones of Saul and Jonathan be disinterred from the desert sands of Jabesh-gilead. These remains were brought back to Saul's home country of Benjamin. Along with all the corpses of the seven young men crucified, they would be given noble and royal burial in the magnificent mausoleum of Kish, Saul's venerable father.

With this done, the famine ended, the autumn rains returned to freshen the land, and once again the Most High could be entreated on behalf of all the destitute people.

The Word of God speaks clearly to all men, not just to David, about the conditions to be met if they wish to enjoy the blessings of God. These benefits were physical, moral and spiritual. Often in Scripture they are referred to as showers of rain: "former rain" and "latter rain." No matter the form in which they fell, all came as gifts from the generous hand of the Most High. They were gracious expressions of His care and provision for those who walked with God in quiet, humble faith, of obedience to His will. (Read prayerfully Leviticus 26:3–5 and 14–20; Isaiah 59:1–8; Hosea 10:12–13.)

At this time of David's restoration to the throne in Israel, he became acutely aware that the greatest need of his nation was not more military power or judicial administration but rather a turning back to God. He had sufficient spiritual perception to recognize that size and scale of state were of no significance to God unless the spirits of the people were in harmony with the wishes of the Most High.

He gives expression to this truth in the magnificent psalm recorded in 2 Samuel 22. There he proclaims boldly without apology to his people that it was the Lord who was his strength and his defense in the dark hours of his storm-tossed reign. His was not a peaceful reign. Far from it, it had been a time of upheaval and unrest both for himself and his people. He was erecting a mighty empire, but it was being built amid bloodshed, violence, intrigue and armed combat.

Still for David in the midst of the mayhem God was—
"my rock"
"my fortress"
"my deliverer"
"my shield"
"my salvation"
"my high tower"
"my refuge—my Savior."

As we gradually approach the closing years of his tempestuous career it becomes ever more obvious that David's preeminent desire was to extol the greatness of God. His most compelling ambition was to exalt the honor of The Eternal One among his people. This became his consuming passion. The days of spear and shield and bugle calls to battle were almost over. Only one or two serious skirmishes remained to be settled with his ancient enemies the giant Philistines from Gath.

David was now almost sixty years old. There were flecks of gray in his beard and around his temples. But still he bore himself with the regal dignity of a man hardened and forged in the fires of combat. He had slain the giant Goliath in the tender years of his youth. He was sure he still had the stamina to slay a second giant now at the advanced age of sixty.

But it was not to be. He came within a hair of being butchered to death by Ishbi-benob, a powerful giant whose spearhead alone weighed almost as much as a sledge hammer. Only the last minute intervention by the stalwart, fearless officer Abishai saved David's life. Abishai, the furious warrior with nerves of tungsten and a temper like a blast furnace, killed the giant on the spot. It was one time he did not wait for David's permission to raise his sword and shatter the enemy's skull.

From that moment on David's loyal men refused adamantly to ever let the aged king accompany them into battle again. Despite his failings, despite his lapses, despite his human weakness, David was still honored and esteemed among his men as *"The light of Israel," "the hope of the nation."* They could and did subdue what remnants remained of the giants of Gath. But it was David who must be preserved to lead them on in the paths of righteousness.

Their monarch was a man who above all else wished to do God's will. He was in truth a man after God's own heart. This they all knew full well—and this they respected.

20

David's Magnificent Psalms and His Heroic Warriors

As the evening shadows of David's declining years cast their ever-lengthening shade across his life, he did not shrink back into oblivion. He would not allow his diminishing physical strength to restrict his enthusiasm for the work of the Lord God. Nor did he permit the pressures of state to stifle his spiritual zest for the exaltation of Jehovah God in the life of Israel.

With great spiritual wisdom, David saw the necessity for a change in his priorities as the long years of his life drew steadily toward the twilight of his times. Now his chief concern was the spiritual growth of his nation rather than its military might or its political power. He was astute enough to realize that if a people truly honored God, He in turn would honor them, lifting them up above the nations around them.

So, as will be seen in subsequent chapters, he was the one who established the spiritual precedent that would serve as a role model for his fellow citizens to emulate. He did not leave this responsibility to the priests or to the prophets. He saw with clear, unclouded, spiritual discernment that he himself had been chosen of God, anointed for service, called to be a king, a shepherd, a psalmist, a priest and a prophet to his people. Nor would he neglect these talents entrusted to him by the Most High.

They were to be exercised and employed not only for his own self-fulfillment as a monarch, who had made his majestic mark in history, but also for the benefit of others. The legacy of his life was a brilliant endowment that enriched all of Israel during his rule, but much more than that, it has been an inspiration to all of God's people of every nation across thousands of years.

We can safely say that not more than half a dozen other men have ever made such a spiritual impact on human history.

It is important that we should understand clearly the secrets of David's success. They are summed up here in precise form, though they have been discussed at length in previous chapters, both in this book and in *David I.* Here they are:

1. David was not perfect. He was not a plaster-cast saint with a halo around his head. He was a passionate man with lights and shadows in his character. But, and that is a very large word just here, he was a man *totally available to God and His purposes.* God has difficulty finding such individuals. Most of us, by a deliberate decision of our wills, refuse to relinquish our rights to the Lord. We insist on controlling our own careers rather than capitulate to the control of Christ.

We are determined to make all our own choices in life, rather than submit in humility to the gracious sovereignty of God's gracious Spirit.

In essence this is personal pride. Such people God resists! It is, therefore, little wonder that the majority of men and women who claim to be God's people achieve little for Him.

2. David, because of his humility and contrite spirit, was sensitive to God's Spirit. He was a man with "a broken heart." That phrase does not mean the center of his emotions had been grieved by sorrow of an intimate sort. In the Scriptures, a "broken heart" is a will that has been trained and disciplined to do God's will. The expression is used in the same sense as we speak of a horse "being broken to the saddle" or an ox "being broken to the plow" or an ass "being broken to bear burdens." It means to be harnessed or yoked.

Our service to the Almighty is not predicated upon some soft, sentimental, fickle, human emotion of a broken heart. Our usefulness is directly dependent on our being disciplined in will and spirit to do God's will no matter what that means.

Our Lord spoke clearly of counting the cost to follow Him—and work with Him. That cost is suffering as He does.

Most modern Christians only look for a comfortable way of life.

They only serve if they happen "to feel like it."

They know little of disciplined devotion to God, even less of literally laying down their lives, their strength, their time, their money or their ambitions for the sake of others.

But David did! He demonstrated this again and again in the life he lived out before his people in his declining years. It was a life of amazing self-sacrifice.

3. David had the remarkable capacity to repent of his wrongs whenever he became acutely aware that he had sinned against God. He was not haughty or arrogant.

He was a man capable of enormous remorse. His outpouring of genuine sorrow for wrongs committed touch us to the depths. He is not given to excuses or putting the blame on others. He knew his personal responsibilities and when he failed in them he took the necessary steps to put things right with God and man.

Such a person the Most High picks up again and again. He restores them to fellowship with Himself! He heals the wounds and reestablishes them in peace and prosperity. He forgives and forgets the failings and folly of the past. He honors such a contrite spirit.

4. Lastly, David realized he was a gifted person. He knew he had been endowed with special talents from God. He refused to bury them in oblivion. He would not neglect them. They were to be used for the honor of God and to bless others. These capacities were not just to advance his own ambitions.

His abilities were bestowed to promote God's purposes upon the planet.

- He was a gifted musician skilled in playing the harp.
- He was a talented composer of psalms, hymns and poems.
- He was an outstanding statesman of great diplomacy.
- He was a fearless, brilliant, military man, a gallant general.
- He was an astute financier who amassed fortunes.
- He was a deep, spiritual person, a true "shepherd" to Israel.
- He was a prophet who spoke for God.

All of these facets of his life are clearly reflected in the two psalms set in juxtaposition in 2 Samuel 22 and 23. The first of these is in fact the same as Psalm 18 in the *Psalter*. It is commonly called *"The Great Psalm."* Quite obviously it was composed early in his youth prior to the time he was driven into exile by Saul's ruthless tyranny.

This magnificent poem is one of adoration and adulation for the Lord. It is an unabashed hymn of praise to the Most High for His part in preserving David during all his dangers. He ascribes to God all the credit and all the honor for his achievements. In it David foretells with the sure accuracy of a prophet all the mighty exploits he will yet accomplish as the leader of his people.

Yet it is without question a psalm written long before David had erred in his ways. It was composed before he had turned to violence, deception and intrigue in his career. In this poem David protests his own innocence. He disclaims any wrongdoing. He declares his own obedience to God's commands, the righteousness of his conduct before the Lord.

It moves us deeply to read such a manifest. For in the light of later events his testimony would change. Even though in those early years, Jonathan would agree and declare to Saul that David was innocent and did only good. Later in life, David would confess openly and freely that he had in fact sinned grievously against God. He would plead for pardon. He would cast himself upon the mercy of the Most High. He would beg that God's gracious Spirit be not taken from him, even though He was so deeply grieved by David's terrible crimes committed against Bath-sheba and Uriah, his loyal officer.

And again, yes again, we are moved to the depths, for David was not alone in his sin. He speaks for all of us, for each of us has a past.

In *2 Samuel 23*, there is recorded what is reputed to be David's last psalm. It takes the form of a prophetic piece in which he states some remarkable and astonishing facts. Of these the most important is the straightforward declaration, *"The Spirit of the Lord spake by me, and his word was in my tongue!" (2 Samuel 23:2).*

This was David's categorical claim to fame as one who foretold the future as surely as the prophets who preceded him. In this very psalm, brief as it is, he proclaims the unbreakable covenant which God would make with him as a king in Israel. This covenant was that his dynasty would endure; that through his lineage a Savior would come; that the Greater David would in due time be the One to rule the entire earth. In all of this the coming of Christ was anticipated.

Proof that such events did indeed take place is provided in the genealogies given to us in the early chapters of both Matthew and Luke (see especially Matthew 1:6 & 17; Luke 1:69).

But beyond even this the numerous predictions which David made in Psalms 16, 22, 23 and 24 regarding the life and death of Christ are convincing evidence of David's major role as a prophet in the history of Israel.

It is astonishing yet wonderful to hear Peter on the day of Pentecost proclaim boldly to the huge crowds in Jerusalem that the very events they witnessed at Christ's crucifixion, death, burial and resurrection were those foretold by David. Unashamedly Peter repeated verbatim the statements made by David over a thousand years before in Psalm 16.

The truth of his prophecy came with such compelling conviction that over 3,000 converts were added to the band of disciples that day. It was the genesis of the New Testament Church. And its very beginning was the inviolate truth written by David under the unction of God's Spirit, so long before.

In the face of all the foregoing, it must be said that David's glory did not lie either in his gifts as a man nor in his genius as a leader. His splendor lay in his willingness to be a servant to his people and to his God. He was in essence a living example of the magnificent grace of God active in the life of a man available to the purposes of the Most High.

What God could do for and through him, He is also able to do for any of us who will give Him the chance. Most of us are too stubborn to submit to His wishes. Then we wonder why our little lives are so useless, so impotent, so unavailing in the economy of Christ.

A great part of the impact of David's character on his contemporaries was its spiritual dimension. Even if some of those near to him, like Joab, were not men of faith in the Almighty, still David's own devotion to Jehovah God commanded their respect. He was not a man to hide his hope in the Lord. Consequently, the men under his command were keenly aware that David himself was a leader under God's command. This in part explains their unflinching loyalty and love to him. This is a unique quality found in very few leaders.

Furthermore, as mentioned before, David in his years of exile under Saul's tyranny had suffered with his people as few rulers ever do. He knew what it was to be oppressed, abused and harassed by those in power. Accordingly he fully understood the feelings and fears of his fellow citizens. He was one with them in this common bond. Very much like this the Greater David, our Beloved Lord Jesus, the Christ, has lived among us, suffered with us and is therefore touched with the feelings of our lot in life.

In truth David was not a monarch aloof from his men of war. He was one of them. He was their adored hero.

It is of more than passing interest to discover that David

187

kept a special honor roll of those warriors who had shown outstanding valor in battle. There was a specific list of men who had demonstrated unusual bravery against the enemy at the utmost risk to their own lives. This heroic group is named in 2 Samuel 23.

The unusual aspect of this honor roll is that its first few illustrious members are named in descending order of their achievements. Adino single-handedly slaughtered eight hundred of the enemy. Eleazer stood almost alone with David on one grim occasion and fought the foe so unrelentingly that his hand was literally locked to his sword. Because of it God gave them a great victory. Then there was Shammah who stood alone in a huge field of lentils and literally defended it single-handedly against the Philistine invaders until the Lord honored him with a tremendous triumph.

Three other gallant fighters broke through the ranks of the Philistines encamped at Bethlehem. Putting their own lives in utter jeopardy, they drew water from the well there to refresh David. He was so touched by their devotion he dared not drink it. It was too precious a sacrament gained by the love of his men to be taken by him. Instead he poured it out as a solemn and sacred oblation to his Lord God. It was an offering of genuine gratitude for the loyalty of his men. This drink of water was much more than water, it was symbolic of the very blood, the very lives of the three men who risked all for their beloved leader.

He had risked his own life often for those under him. David was not an "arm chair" commander. He was not a "behind-the-battlelines" general. He had been in the very thick of things again and again, fighting alongside his men. Now they in turn were not reluctant to risk themselves for his honor and for his glory.

This was a part of the secret of David's success as a military leader. He knew many of his men by name. He had slept under the stars with them on stony, thorny ground. He had tramped long miles with them on some very tough desert marches. He had stood shoulder to shoulder with them in bloody combat where no one dared to turn and flee for their own safety. Like roaring lions they had attacked the enemies of Israel, then blown the battle bugles to signal great victories.

David knew all about what it was to swing a sword, to smell the heady, sickening stench of blood and death— to hear the groans of men wounded and gored with spears, to be so weary with war and battle fatigue that the eyes glazed over and the muscles screamed for relief. He had been through a hundred skirmishes on the desert sands. He knew all about the brutalizing effect of combat on those under him. Still he loved them.

In his ranks there had also been men like his ruthless nephew Abishai, so fearless, so daring, so eager "to mix it" with the enemy. Single-handedly, he had killed over three hundred men in battle. There was Benaiah who had such a long combat record it could not be repeated. Not only had he faced lionlike men from Moab all alone, but like David he had with his bare hands killed a lion in winter. He had done the same with a formidable Egyptian fighter. And there had been the swift-footed Asahel, so athletic, so fearless, who alas fell on Abner's spear and was killed.

Besides all of these special heroes, David had a prize list of thirty other men who had reached positions of great honor and adulation in his esteem. He may not have pinned *purple hearts* or *Victoria Crosses* to their tunics, but he recognized their loyalty and valor for all time, by inscribing their names on his roll of honor.

Among those included in that royal scroll was one by the name of *Uriah the Hittite*, never to be forgotten! One whose memory had been branded indelibly on the conscience of David's sensitive spirit.

21

David's Evil Census and Ornan's Generous Spirit

David's affection for his fighting men, commendable as it was, also served as a subtle temptation to his own spiritual well-being. This is not unusual in the affairs of those entrusted with leadership and positions of power. It has often been said that *"power corrupts."* And in truth there are not many human beings who can handle wealth, authority, power or prominence without falling prey to its corroding pride.

The king's own magnificent military exploits and campaigns had been so closely intertwined with those of his men at arms that they moved as a single unit. It was this military power which had been used so effectively to build his mighty empire. And even though in his writings and oratory David was careful to give the Most High honor and credit for his victories, he was nevertheless still human enough to put confidence in the strength of his fighting forces.

When, after his return to the throne in Jerusalem, he decided to consolidate his hold on the kingdom, he made the unwise decision to register all the men of military

191

age. Without question he was sure this was a shortcut to bringing the entire nation into subservience to his command. It may have appeared to him to be an astute military move, especially since a census of this sort would give him precise information on Israel's military might. But from God's perspective it was terrible folly. More than that, it was an act of insubordination to His Divine Majesty.

The reader may have difficulty understanding this.

Up until the rule of Saul and David as Israel's first kings, the nation had been a *Theocracy* directly under divine authority, governed by God Almighty. It was He who had led them, won their battles over the enemy, and eventually endowed them with prestige and power in their land of plenty.

Yet Israel, a perverse and petulant people, were not content with this divine arrangement. They insisted on having a human monarchy. Samuel, the ancient seer and last of the judges, warned the obdurate people that they were sinning grievously against the Lord, Jehovah, in demanding a king with a human dynasty. As a prophet of the Most High, Samuel predicted with great accuracy the oppression Israel would endure under her kings. They would pay dearly with intense hardships for their choice of human sovereigns.

To quote him verbatim he declared, "He [the king] will take your menservants and your maidservants and your goodliest young men and your asses, and put them to his work. . . ." (read 1 Samuel 8:1–22).

Now that very thing was being done by David. He was not about to be deflected from his determination. Joab, to whom the responsibility fell to register the nation, pled with David to reconsider his action. But the king was adamant and refused to relent. He was turning to human resources for appraising his power, rather than relying on the mighty arm of God.

This enraged Joab, who, in one of the few flashes of spiritual perception he ever showed, reminded the king that he now enjoyed the full loyalty of the whole nation, even if it increased ten times ten. It was a great evil to take this census. God would be grieved and all would suffer.

David, becoming old and set in his ways, persisted!

Joab went off in a huff, bitter in spirit, reluctant to make the register, but doing it anyway to appease the king. Perhaps he was afraid of being demoted in rank again. But his heart was not in this miserable assignment.

He had counted roughly one and a half million men of military age when the Lord decided to intervene. He was highly displeased with what was being done in Israel.

Even the people themselves should have had backbone enough to refuse the register. But like stupid sheep they dumbly submitted to this indignity. Perhaps they, too, thought it a brilliant idea to assess their military might— as mere men—apart from God. At any rate, the census was never completed. Two tribes still remained to be enumerated by Joab when it was clear judgment would fall on the nation. Because of this, concise numbers were never recorded, leaving the exact outcome confused as the various accounts clearly indicate.

The aged and venerated prophet Gad was to be the spokesman for the Most High in this dark and troubled hour. The first time he had come to David was almost forty years before when David had hidden himself in the cave of Adullam, in exile from Saul. Now again the fearless prophet came to the king in his hour of peril. His message from the Most High was ominous and frightening.

David had transgressed grievously. All of Israel had been led into serious insubordination. Dire discipline must follow. The king could have his choice of severe and stern correction:

1. *Another three years of famine.*
2. *Three months of invasion by cruel enemy forces.*
3. *Three days of divine judgment.*

Whichever course he chose, the king knew full well that the loss of life would be staggering. He and his people would pass through appalling suffering. In his stubborn folly he had sinned grievously against God. It was inevitable the consequences for his misconduct must be faced. He was reaping the cruel and harsh out-working of his wickedness. Because of his own perverseness he would have to bear the awesome burden of seeing men and women perish. What should he do? He could not escape the inviolate principle of cause and effect.

In frantic desperation David, his face pale and drawn, flung himself upon the mercy of God. He whispered to Gad, in stark terror: *"Let me fall now into the hand of the LORD; for very great are his mercies. . . ."*

As pointed out in previous chapters, David had the remarkable capacity to clearly see his sin against God and men. He was an individual sensitive in spirit who was willing to confess his wrongs and repent of his willful wickedness. But as he grew older his conscience seemed to be slower to respond to the rebuke of those God sent to warn him of his waywardness. It was almost as if he was slowing down spiritually as well as physically and mentally (see Ecclesiastes 4:13).

The reason for saying this was that some seventy thousand choice young men perished with pestilence throughout the nation before David actually prostrated himself before the Lord. Only when the destroying angel, who had wiped out all the firstborn in Egypt and in Pharaoh's palace, now stood over Jerusalem ready to ravage it, did David and his elders realize fully in what peril they stood.

Clothed in sackcloth and ashes, the king and his counselors collapsed to the floor, their faces to the ground. They had actually seen the angel of death, suspended in space above the city, with sword drawn, at the point of bringing dreadful destruction to the royal city. In a matter of moments every man, woman and child in Jerusalem could have been wiped out.

It was then, and only then, that the king cried out in intense contrition for mercy from the Most High. Already multitudes of his people had paid the supreme price for this great evil in the nation. Only if God restrained His hand could a total catastrophe be averted. The awful consequences of David's wrong were being worked out.

David cried out in anguish to God and said, *"Is it not I that commanded the people to be numbered? Even I it is that have sinned and done evil indeed; but as for these sheep, what have they done? Let thine hand, I pray thee, Oh LORD my God, be on me, and on my father's house; but not on thy people that they should be plagued."*

If more men and women truly saw the gravity of their sins against God, they would desist from evil. But they do not. A large portion of the responsibility for sin being so rampant in our society is that our leaders will not cry out against it. Rather, they merely protest with pious platitudes that people are "sick," that they "hurt," and what they need is soft sympathy, rather than deep heart-changing repentance.

Amid the awesome mayhem, death and destruction

in Israel, with death and anguish on every side, God beheld a man—a solitary, ordinary man, doing an ordinary job in a very ordinary way. This man possessed a most extraordinary spirit. His name was Ornan, otherwise called Araunah.

He was not even a Hebrew. He was not descended from Abraham, Isaac or Jacob. He was a Jebusite whose ferocious forebears had occupied Jerusalem for hundreds of years until it was subdued by Joab under David's command.

Like his forefathers he had continued to live in the royal city now occupied by the Israelis. Apparently he had given his allegiance not only to David but also to Jehovah God, as the Lord Most High in his life.

On this ominous day, Ornan was driving his oxen back and forth, round and round, across his threshing floor. The team and the heavy threshing sledge they hauled were beating out the grain amid a cloud of dust and chaff that hung heavy in the hot air. It all seemed so matter of fact, so common, so conventional in that culture.

Yet, strange to say, it was precisely at that site where the destroying angel suddenly stopped. For there God by His Spirit saw more than a common farmer threshing his grain. He saw into the soul of a simple man who was utterly open and available to the purposes of God for him and his adopted people.

Ornan was covered with dust and chaff. It stuck in his hair. It clung to the sticky sweat on his chest and face and legs and arms. He was not beautiful to behold. But he was beautiful within.

He had four stalwart, sturdy sons. When the farm lads saw the angel standing at the edge of the threshing floor, in fear they scrambled for safety. What did this mean? They would soon find out!

196

For in the meantime the prophet Gad had already arrived at the royal palace with a message for David from the Most High. He was to rush out at once and erect a temporary altar on Ornan's threshing floor, there to offer an appropriate sacrifice of oxen as a sin offering for himself and his people. Only this could now propitiate for the sins of the whole nation. There was to be no delay. There was no time for David to travel to the tabernacle at Gibeon outside the city.

David did not hesitate an instant. He dared not ask God any questions. Time was of the essence. What God said he would do. His life and that of all his people hung on his implicit and prompt obedience to the Lord's commands.

In a matter of minutes the king, all draped in sackcloth, ashes on his head, dust on his feet and hands, stood facing Ornan, who in turn was all covered in chaff and dust. These two men, looking like a couple of wild and unkempt scarecrows, engaged in one of the most titanic transactions in all of human history. God uses some of the most unlikely settings and unusual people to achieve His greatest ends.

The contrite monarch, red-eyed with weeping, bowed in spirit, asked Ornan to sell him his threshing floor as a site for sacrifice to save his people. He could easily have commandeered it in this national emergency. But David was too great-hearted for that, too generous in soul, too sensitive in spirit toward his Jebusite neighbor. No, he would purchase it for a handsome price.

Ornan's reply is utterly breath-taking! It stands as one of the most magnificent statements ever made by a man! It is a declaration of such spiritual splendor it stirs us to the depths!!

It also lifts us to great heights of awe and respect.

197

In the plain language of a plain man, yet transmitting the impact and power of divine approbation, Ornan smiled and said: *"My LORD, the king, do whatever you see best. I give you my threshing floor. I give you my oxen for the burnt offering. I give you all my wooden tools and sledge to use for fuel to offer the sacrifice in this spot. I give it all, to you and to my God!"*

There simply was no holding back of anything.

There was no excuse that it would ruin his livelihood.

There was no protest about how to support his family.

This was complete and immediate abandonment to the will and wishes of God. It was whole-hearted relinquishment of all he possessed for the purposes of the Most High. It was pure, undefiled self-sacrifice for the good of others.

David was so deeply moved by Ornan's gesture he paid him six hundred shekels of gold. The equivalent value in today's currency at time of writing is about $137,000. The king refused to offer a sacrifice that cost him nothing. But by far the greater offer of a sacrifice of supreme worth had been made by this ordinary man, Ornan, doing an ordinary job, but whose will was set above all else to do God's will, in an extraordinary way.

Wonder of wonders, that special spot was the very site on Mount Moriah where Abraham had offered his son Isaac to God, 850 years before! Marvel of marvels, it was the very spot where Solomon would later erect the most beautiful temple ever to grace the earth! How God exalts those who honor Him!

One ordinary man's generosity to God and quiet trust that He did all things well ended in the salvation of his nation and great honor to his God. All the rest of Israel was spared that day!

True sacrifice never comes out of our surplus. It comes out of that which costs us the risk of all we have for the sake of others. It is laying down our lives, our time, our talents, our means on the line.

Most people positively refuse to risk anything for the Lord. Then they wonder why their lives are so drab and sterile. The average North American with all his/her affluence gives less than 3 percent to God or charity!!

There is no need to say more!

22

David Prepares for the Temple

Because of the spectacular salvation accorded to all of Israel at Ornan's threshing floor, David decided at once it was the proper site on which a magnificent temple should be erected. Also this spot on Mount Moriah, so sacred in the traditions of Israel, because of Abraham's encounter with God there, was well suited for special honor to the Most High (see 2 Chronicles 3:1).

As pointed out in a previous chapter, the building of a beautiful edifice to the glory of God was not an idea unique to David. It would be likened to a national dream for Israel since the days of Samuel the prophet. But it was David who began to give form and substance to this hope and aspiration. Now that his people had become stabilized as a formidable empire in the Middle East, the trauma of war and the upheavals of inner conflicts were pretty well passed. Israel was ready for the spiritual stability which a magnificent temple could represent. The nomadic days were done. The constant shift of a mobile tabernacle needed to be supplanted with a structure that was more permanent.

David Prepares for the Temple

Jehovah God, who had first given the detailed design of the original tabernacle made of skins, staves and sturdy curtains, was not averse to the erection of an imposing building of stone, cedar and gold. In fact in due time it was the Lord Himself who would again give David, just as He did Moses, all the precise plans for its layout and construction. What the Eternal One did object to was that the actual construction should be defiled by the hands of a king whose career had been stained with so much bloodshed.

It was the divine desire, made clear to David, that his successor, a man of peace, should build the temple in a time of peace, in order that it should usher in an era of peace for His people.

It is a great tribute to the character of David that he did not take umbrage at this arrangement of his affairs. He did not go into a sulk or angry diatribe against God for not granting him this great honor at the end of his life. Nor was he the least bit jealous of his son Solomon who would gain enduring glory through the project. Rather, David gladly accepted the Lord's decree and still threw his enormous energy and expertise into preparations for the temple. This generous attitude and gracious spirit of wholehearted support stand as a great and noble monument to the memory of this man.

In his stormy career and dappled character, this lingers as one of the most charming chapters in David's life. It lifts him far above the ordinary person and we are given a clear view of a beautiful aspect of his conduct before God and men. It reveals to us a leader of enormous enthusiasm for the honor of his God. Yet he was at the same time a statesman of keen financial skills combined with unusual economic acumen.

All of this was grounded in David's spiritual sensitivity

to the Spirit of God. It was God who in His gracious sovereignty selected Solomon to be David's successor to the throne. When this second child was born to Bath-sheba he was called *Solomon—The Peacable One*. Even Nathan, the prophet, who had brought David such dire news before about the death of Bath-sheba's first boy, brought the great good news that this lad was *Jedidiah— Beloved of the LORD*.

Now the youth was about seventeen years old when David summoned him into his presence. At the early age when most teenagers are tearing around throwing off parental authority and rebelling against any restrictions, David was laying upon his son one of the weightiest responsibilities ever given to a youth of these tender years.

It was Solomon who must take up the task, in concert with his father, of preparing for and building the temple.

It was not an easy assignment. Altogether it would take roughly fourteen years to accomplish. Seven of those would be taken up with meticulous gathering of materials and preparation of the component parts. The other seven years would be consumed in its actual construction on the site selected by David. It must always be borne in mind that each detail was in accord with divine design and in compliance with specific spiritual requirements which have never attended any other building in history.

The exact blueprints and plans were given directly to David by God. They could not be altered or adjusted or modified by human design to compensate for human error. Secondly the entire edifice was to be built in complete silence, without the single sound of a hammer, axe, adze or metal tool upon it. No small feat! One which no contractor in the world today would undertake at any price—even with cost overruns! (See 1 Kings 6:7 and 1 Chronicles 28:10–12.)

For long, long years David had kept the dream of this splendid sanctuary burning brightly in his spirit. He never allowed it to grow dim. Despite all of his troubles—his family feuds, his civil conflicts, his wider wars with other nations—the collection of materials for the temple had gone on steadily. It was as if the temple was the lodestar at the end of his life that drew all of his energies to itself with relentless magnetism and undeviating direction.

He opened huge quarries under the very city of Jerusalem where magnificent white limestone could be precut in huge blocks to exactly fit the temple. These were later called *"The Cotton Caves,"* they were so white. From among the many alien residents within his far-flung empire, he recruited skilled artisans to work in stone. They worked with incredible skill in the darkness below ground, their only light coming from crude oil lamps. Deep underground not a single stroke of a stone-cutting tool was heard up above.

The king had also assembled colossal quantities of iron, brass and bronze. It would be impossible even to guess how many tons of this material was in storage ready to be used for bolts, bars, nails, hinges, beams and ornate ornamentation throughout the sanctuary.

Traditionally Israel had very few craftsmen skilled in the smelting and shaping of these metals. So again David, with astute foresight and meticulous planning, arranged for fine and experienced metal workers to be gathered from the foreign craftsmen scattered across his empire. They would be able to contribute the finest workmanship in all the world to his project.

Much the same preparation had gone into supplying

cedar wood for the inner walls of the temple. This came from the high mountains of Lebanon. The trees had to be cut in the high country, hauled down to the sea, then shipped along the coast in booms, to be cut into suitable lumber closer to the building site. It was a prodigious project, made possible because of David's firm friendship with Hiram king of Tyre.

Cedar was highly esteemed because of its beautiful grain, its delicate aroma and its imperviousness to insects or decay. David had enormous piles of this lumber prepared. As a matter of interest, at one stage no fewer than 80,000 men were engaged in just securing timber for the temple.

Even this pales into relative insignificance when we consider what this remarkable man had achieved in gathering up gold and silver for the glory of God. He told Solomon he had on hand at least 100,000 talents of gold stored in his royal vaults.

In terms of 1986 currency values, that is roughly 67 billion dollars.

His hoard of silver was over a million talents.

In equivalent terms of our money, that is 18 billion dollars.

In short David had a national surplus of 85 billions!

The United States at this writing has a deficit of 256 billions.

Besides these precious metals, no exact figures are even supplied for the incredible store of precious stones, rare draperies and exquisite fine furnishings that had been gathered for this magnificent building. A conservative guess and most modest appraisal would put a minimum value of at least one hundred billion dollars on the total accumulation of material David had on hand, ready for Solomon to take over.

David Prepares for the Temple

It is all the more remarkable to realize that David had managed to achieve this during the long trying years of his troubled rule. When most nations go deep into debt during times of war, he had the economic genius to achieve enormous financial wealth while also building an empire. Few men in human history could claim such a monumental accomplishment.

In large part, the supreme secret of his success in this area of his life was his intense devotion to God. David truly loved the Lord. God was preeminent in his affections and loyalty. Though he had serious lapses in his spiritual pilgrimage with the Almighty, never, ever, did he allow that to deflect him from his burning, all-consuming desire to do God's will and to bring Him honor above all else.

In his own rough and ready way, David was utterly convinced that the construction of a glorious temple was the highest honor he could bestow on the Lord. He was determined to actually do something beautiful for God. It was not enough for him to merely sing great psalms or compose marvelous music to the honor of his God. He longed to leave behind him—in tangible form of stone, wood, gold, silver and precious stones—a fitting sanctuary for the Most High whom he worshiped and adored.

Nor was he remiss in instilling this same enthusiasm and ambition in his young son Solomon. He used every possible means open to him to inspire the young prince to catch the vision of what he could do to exalt the Most High.

It was in fact an exact parallel to the clear instructions given to us by God's Spirit in the New Testament: We as *"temples of the Holy Spirit"* should see to it that our characters are constructed of such fine and goodly materials (qualities) that they shall endure to the honor of God (see 1 Corinthians 3:19–17 & 6:19–20).

Over and over David reassured Solomon of the marvelous promises which God had given him on his behalf. Here they are in concise and categorical statements:

"He will be my son.
I shall be his father.
I will establish his kingdom.
I will be with him and prosper him.
I will give him wisdom and understanding.
I will bless him in building my temple.
I will give him peace and rest.
I will give him courage and strength."

The only conditions Solomon had to meet to enjoy all these magnificent benefits from the Most High are the same ones we must meet:

Quietly put complete confidence in God.
Simply comply with His commands in love.
Set our wills to do God's will in every event.
Quietly go out in the world and do His bidding.

For young Solomon this meant carrying through on the construction of the temple, no matter how difficult and involved such an assignment might seem to one so youthful and inexperienced. The supreme truth above all others which David endeavored to impress on his son was *"God is here, with you! All is well!"*

In addition to this stirring spiritual encouragement that the king gave to his son, he took some significant practical steps to assure him of support from the people.

The first of these was to summon the other princes into his presence. Instead of rivalry, jealousy and jockeying for power, they were to rally around Solomon and give him their loyal support as the new sovereign. Most of them appeared to comply with David's commands, except for Adonijah, who, at the very end of the aged monarch's life, devised a scheme whereby he might usurp the throne and displace Solomon. Fortunately this conspiracy was aborted.

The next astonishing step that David took was to actually abdicate the throne, transferring the monarchy to his son (1 Chronicles 23:1). This was a wise and benevolent transfer of power and authority that would enable the youth to carry out the heavy responsibilities entrusted to him.

The scriptural record does not give the precise details of exactly how this was done. It appears that in certain areas of leadership during the last few years of his long life, David still ruled as a co-regent with his son. Privately David transferred enormous power to Solomon. Yet in public the nation still recognized David as their king.

Proof of this lay in the fact that on at least three occasions Solomon was crowned king with a public coronation. So he is probably the only monarch in history who was made king three times over.

Certainly when it came to spiritual leadership, it was David who provided the impetus and inspiration for Israel. He most definitely did not abdicate his divine responsibilities in this respect.

He was wise enough to see that the mere erection of a grand structure to the glory of God was not sufficient in itself. The temple would have to be properly tended by a priesthood of comparable splendor and honor. The honor of the Most High demanded more than an edifice of stone, wood and gold. It required the constant commitment of those who carried out its special services with devotion in disciplined dignity.

To this end David commanded that all the Levites be

mustered for temple duty. There were 38,000 of them appointed to this sacred service. From the most prominent of their leaders to the least known of their youth, all over thirty years of age, each was assigned special responsibility in his service for the Lord.

These were all arranged carefully into rotating shifts, so that nothing was left to chance. There would always be a full staff on duty to carry out the functions of the temple, as well as serve the needs of those who came there to offer sacrifices or worship the Lord God.

This division of responsibility is very revealing. It discloses how concerned David was to see that the temple did indeed become the nerve center of the nation, that his own palace and throne were not the true power center of the people. Rather, the direction of their destiny and the permanence of their empire was governed and grounded in this superb and noble sanctuary of The Eternal One.

24,000 Levites were to carry out regular temple duties.

6,000 Levites were to serve as judges and ministers.

4,000 Levites were responsible for maintenance services.

4,000 Levites were to provide music, psalms and praise.

This latter aspect was one to which David gave great prominence. He never forgot or neglected his own remarkable gifts of music. So he made sure the temple and its elaborate courtyards would resound with the melodies of magnificent orchestras, bands, choirs and combined groups who gave gratitude, adulation and praise to God.

Nor were these to be sporadic sessions. The giving of thanks and the singing of psalms in public worship was to be done every morning and every evening. There was to be a sweet savor of music and song and adoration rising to the Lord just as surely and constantly as there arose a flame of fire on the altar of sacrifice which was never to go out or be extinguished.

The presence, the power, the person of the Most High was not only manifest in the flame of fire but also in the *paean of praise* that rose day and night from His people.

What was true for the temple then should be true today for each of us who are the temple of God's Spirit today. Within us there should be the unquenched fire of His presence, while rising from within comes endless loyalty, gratitude and praise to Him who loves us!

23

David As an Administrator

To be a great king in Israel, the national leader had to have wide interests touching upon all the diverse aspects of national life. These were more than just political or military responsibilities. They covered the whole range of internal administration, spiritual supervision, financial affairs and agricultural production.

Fortunately for the burgeoning empire, David was an individual of enormous administrative ability. Without doubt this unusual capacity was a special gift with which he had been endowed by God. He was a man of broad horizons, the long view, and contagious enthusiasm to carry out far-reaching schemes.

As we study the scriptural record given to us by God's Spirit, it is fascinating to discover how David actually delegated authority and gave special responsibility to those under him. It was not done by the creation of committees or the election of officers. Rather, the process was one of allowing the Lord God to make the selection on the basis of drawn lots which were linked directly to the priesthood. In other words, though Israel was no longer a theocracy, it still was a nation which recognized the supreme sovereignty of God and relied for its choice of leadership at all levels of government on His direction rather than the wisdom of men.

The final choice of those who would administer the temple, or govern in the provinces, or dispense justice, or provide leadership in music or care for agricultural production, was done by lot. Even the rotation of service and the regular, smooth transition of responsibility from month to month was carried out on the basis of divine direction exercised through the drawing of lots.

This was the procedure Joshua had established with such remarkable success when he administered Israel with the strong spiritual guidance given to him by Eleazar the high priest.

There is no doubt David endeavored to administer the nation in the same way in his day. Coupled with this spiritual concept of divine authority in the affairs of state, were the remarkable opportunities given to the ordinary person for service. Again and again the point is made that great and small, experienced and inexperienced individuals could contribute to the national good.

David's own spectacular career was living evidence of what God could do with an obscure person who to his contemporaries may have seemed of no consequence. A mere shepherd boy, who was despised even by his own brothers, had, under God's great hand, brought his people to a position of formidable power in the then known world. What the Most High had done with him, David was sure He could do with anyone available to His purposes. So in a delightful way he saw to it that everyone in his kingdom was given equal opportunity to do something great and beautiful for God and man.

The much vaunted concepts of liberty, equality and

freedom of action were not something unique to the founding fathers of the American Republic. Those values had been clearly grasped and instituted by David nearly 2,790 years before the Declaration of Independence. One of the great tragedies of our times is that to a large degree this aspect of freedom for all has become twisted and torn by political manipulation, the power of lobbying by vested interests and the gross corruption of those in office who use political patronage for their own ends. The double tragedy is that much of this maneuvering is linked to wealth, not to divine direction. Little wonder nations flounder and fall prey to insidious forces within their body politic.

The astonishing thing is David even used the same means of selecting musicians, vocalists and instrumentalists in the temple ceremonies. Specially gifted performers were given no preference.

The modern church would do well indeed to pay special attention to the statements made here regarding the role of music in the sanctuary of the Most High. Very clearly it is stated that even those who play instruments as well as those who sing should do so for three main purposes:

1) To praise, honor and extol the Lord God.
2) To serve God's people in this admonition of praise.
3) To prophesy—i.e., to tell forth the message and truths that God wishes to give His people.

In other words, the primary function of music was to exalt God and to uplift His people with His truth.

Much of the music provided in the church today does not do this. It has been so infiltrated by the vain philosophy of the world that it is used as a medium either to glamorize the performer or to lightly entertain the audience. The aura of the night club and the glitter of the television stage have swept into the sanctuary. The same subtle tempos, the same hard rock rhythms, the same nasal whines, the same bodily contortions used by the most diabolical worldly music-makers are copied by Christians.

It is noteworthy, too, that the musicians in David's reign were carefully instructed in the songs of the Lord. They were taught to memorize the great psalms and magnificent hymns of praise. These were then to be sung to the people so that they in turn would be instructed in truth of eternal worth.

In his own psalms David had dealt with all the glorious aspects of his God: As Creator, as a guardian to His people, as their Redeemer, as the One who could preserve them in all adversity, as their Shepherd. There, too, he gave profound truths as to how God's people should walk with Him in humility and contrition. He tells how we can invest our total confidence in Him. He leads us to see that the whole of life is grounded in God. Bless His name forever and forever!

To his great credit, David did not confine himself, even though so musical, only to artistic interests in his administration. We find him taking great pains to see to the financial affairs of his state. He was especially keen to build up the "temple fund." As mentioned earlier, this was a national dream that had been under way since the days of Samuel the seer. For roughly seventy-five years, it had been added to by such unexpected contributors as Saul, Abner and even Joab the ruthless warrior chief.

Now that the total wealth accumulated was nearly one hundred billion dollars, it required the administration and control of men skilled in accounting. Treasurers, accountants and bookkeepers were as much a part of the national scene as they are today.

When it came to military matters David needed no one to tell him that he was responsible for national defense and the military might of the nation. He had made one serious mistake in registering the available manpower of his people. Still that did not deter him from establishing a standing peacetime army of 288,000 men. They were battle trained, fully equipped, on constant call. They rotated duty every month with 24,000 men on full alert for any crisis. The Swiss form of national preparedness closely resembles David's military strategy. Little wonder Hitler never even dared to try and invade that tough little territory in World War II.

In the area of agriculture, David, because of his own rural background and upbringing, took great interest in all that pertained to crops, soil, livestock and food production. He was intelligent enough to grasp that it was the farmers on the land who ultimately put food on the table for the nation.

Unlike the way it is in our society, land operators were highly esteemed in Israel's culture. Much of their law was linked to the concept of respecting the land and its capacity to provide for its people. It was originally a divine idea that "the land does not belong to us, but rather we belong to the land."

Land was something to be handled with reverence and wisdom. It was to be rotated with various crops. It was to be rested periodically. It was to be sustained with care. All of this has pretty well passed into oblivion on this continent where land is regarded by a greedy society as an expendable commodity which can be ravaged at will by anyone wealthy enough to buy a chunk of it.

Undoubtedly, too, David was astute enough to know

and realize that almost all of his most illustrious predecessors were men of the land. Abraham, Isaac, Jacob, Moses and Gideon were all men who had lived close to the land. It may seem strange, but is nevertheless true, that all through history many great, noble, fine men and women had their early roots in the soil. So losing farms and farmers as we do today is much more than losing a way of life to multinational corporations. It is also to lose the seedbed from which spring some of our finest people.

David knew this with a deep and sure intuition.

So in his administration those on the land were given his own special consideration. They were not thrown to the wind. Little wonder that because of all this his empire stood now, at the end of his life, at the pinnacle of her power. Never again would her splendor exceed that of his day. Solomon's rule may have been more spectacular and glamorous than his father's, but it never equaled the power and might of David's empire.

Because of Solomon's deliberate disobedience to the Word of the Lord in marrying pagan wives and offering sacrifices to their pagan gods, the kingdom was eventually torn from his grasp. Thus, in only one generation, the grandeur and glory of Israel as a mighty empire would be blown to the winds of the world.

There can be no doubt whatsoever that David had a powerful premonition this might happen. He had seen Saul cast aside by the Most High for his disobedience. It might just as easily happen to his own son, Solomon. As with all human beings he was but clay, so easily shaped by circumstances, so readily ruined by self-indulgence.

To try and forestall this from happening David now ordered that all the princes, leaders, chiefs and prominent people from every tribe be assembled in Jerusalem. He had a special pronouncement which he wished to make publicly so that the entire nation would know his intentions. The intense excitement that this generated was like an electrical charge surging through the entire society.

Where before he had given Solomon the serious charge of constructing the temple in a private, personal way as father to son, now David wished to repeat it in public so the whole nation could participate in the project. Almost verbatim, word for word, sentence by sentence, David stood before the gigantic assembly and told them of his own profound longing to construct a house of worship to the honor of Jehovah God.

Without rancor or jealousy he stated that because of his own atrocities in battle and bloodshed he was not to be the builder. Rather, God Himself had chosen the young prince, Solomon, to be his successor and the one responsible for building the temple.

He then turned to Solomon who stood beside him in the position of power and admonished him again of his solemn obligations to comply constantly with God's commands. In forthright language David warned the young man not to forsake the Most High lest he be cast off forever.

Then in the most courageous terms possible he told him to be of great courage and not to fear. God would never fail him if he sought Him diligently. Then as if to cap it all off, he summed up his charge with the stabbing sentence, *"Be strong and do it!"*

It was a highly charged, emotional moment.

But its impact was even more intense when in full view of all assembled David handed to his son rolled scrolls on which were inscribed all of the exact building plans for the temple and its courts. These were drawn to exact scale. They covered every detail of the building and its furnishings.

Without pride or pomp the king announced that all the plans had been given to him with meticulous precision by the gracious Spirit of God. Quite obviously this had only been possible as David spent much time alone in quiet meditation before the presence of the Most High. There in solitude, seeking the mind of God, there had been impressed upon his spirit every exact aspect of the building.

This stands as one of the most remarkable architectural achievements of all time. David was not an architect by training, yet in His sovereign wisdom and generosity God gave him the precise plans for the most beautiful building human hands would ever erect on earth.

A gasp of wonder, awe and joyous astonishment must have risen from the assembled crowd.

But David, the elder statesman, the warrior hero, the empire builder was not through.

He had a second collection of scrolls, almost more astonishing and unbelievable than the first with the building plans. On these were given in minute detail the exact quantities of stone, lumber, gold, silver, bronze, brass and semiprecious stones required for each facet of the building project. Not a thing was omitted. The precise requirements for even the porches, the lavish furnishings and ornate coverings were all included.

There was not to be an ounce of waste or a single error in judgment. All the data needed to do the job was there!

Again in quiet humility, without fanfare or ostentation, David simply assured Solomon that *"All this information the LORD made me understand in writing by His hand upon me—even all the works of this pattern."*

A thundering, rolling, growing cheer of applause must have risen into the summer sky over Jerusalem that day. God, very God, had indeed made known every possible weight and measure for the construction of the temple. Not a single item was left to chance, not a single design was subject to human error.

Even the finest of our engineering firms, using the most sophisticated computer technology, could not come up with an achievement of this caliber. Like the construction of the tabernacle under Moses, this was a classic case of divine design far surpassing anything human skill or ingenuity could devise.

The grisled old king, now in his late sixties, perhaps stooped a little with the long years, stood straight and staunch before his people. He was not done yet. A gentle smile crossed his rugged features.

Turning again to Solomon, he swept his arms across the crowd and declared proudly: "Look, there are all the Levites and the priests delegated to carry out their temple duties. There are all the national leaders who will give you their unstinting support in this great project. There are all the craftsmen, tradesmen and skilled artisans who can carry out the exact construction of this glorious edifice!"

There was a moment's pause. David ran his eyes quickly, searchingly over the assembly: *"Solomon, my son, whom alone God has chosen, is young and tender, and the work is great: for the palace [temple] is not for man, but for the LORD God!"*

At once the assembled leaders and craftsmen caught their monarch's vision. This was for God's glory—not a man's! They would work for it with a will.

24
David's Abounding Joy Because of Israel's Generosity

The events described for us in 1 Chronicles 29 stand as the supreme spiritual pinnacle of David's earthly pilgrimage. It is a pity that the narrative of his illustrious life did not end just there. But to be true to the scriptural record it must be otherwise, as will be shown in the two final chapters of his career.

Still David deserves our honor, respect and applause for the magnificent achievements given to us here. Not only because he managed to unify the entire nation in its determination to build the national dream, but even more so because in a unique and special way he united them to the Most High under the youthful leadership of Solomon.

It must have stunned and surprised those present when David now turned to face them and in most exuberant enthusiasm described all that had been done to gather building materials for the temple. Many from the outlying regions may only have heard vague rumors of just how much incredible wealth was represented by the stone, timber, iron, brass, bronze, gold, silver, precious and semiprecious stones accumulated.

David made no bones about the fact that all during his reign this had been one of his foremost concerns. He had applied all his might and influence to the project. He declared without a hint of embarrassment that he had centered his affection on the preparation of everything needed for the temple. Because he loved the Lord so much and was constrained by such deep gratitude for His care, the least he could do was reciprocate in kind.

Would to God more Christians were so compelled by their love for Christ. What incredible things the church could accomplish in our weary old world!

To demonstrate to his people the depths of his devotion to Jehovah God, David then declared openly, without any fanfare or theatrics, exactly what he himself was giving to God. He was not trying to be sensational. He was being utterly sincere in setting a stirring example before the entire nation.

The gesture staggers us. The figures in modern day terms make many of our great drives look like child's play.

In gold of Ophir alone he donated 115 tons.

In the finest refined silver he gave 265 tons.

What he could have held onto for himself and his enormous family as an estate he gave freely and gladly to the work of the Lord.

Without waiting for any applause or approbation from his audience, the tough old warrior king faced them calmly with set jaw and flashing eyes. Then there rumbled from his chest the challenge that would bring them all roaring to their feet: *"Who then is willing to consecrate his service this day unto the LORD?"*

The stabbing question was met with an electrifying

response. In wild enthusiasm and unbounded joy the leaders from every level of the nation shouted out loud what they were prepared to give. The spontaneous outpouring which flooded from the families of Israel was a spectacle that has never been duplicated at any one time in human history.

The desire, the compelling desire, to just do something magnificent for the Most High swept across the crowd. It loosened purse strings; it loosened heart strings; and it set the people to singing and chanting with pure joy.

Gold, silver, brass, iron, jewelry, precious stones, all hoarded for years, were suddenly released into the hands of the Almighty. Conservatively estimated, the value exceeded four *billion* dollars.

Utter consecration to the Most High is a stirring impulse that moves men to the depths. On this day everyone present knew they had witnessed a scene that would never be repeated. At no time in all of her weary, wayward history had Israel poured out such lavish honor, wealth and praise upon her Redeemer and Preserver.

The ecstatic joy among the people, the hilarious enthusiasm in their giving, the glad abandonment of their savings and wealth to God was all done with such cheerful spontaneity and incredible good will that the very gates of glory must have reverberated with joy. For our Lord loves a cheerful, joyous, hearty giver.

Dear old David was simply beside himself with exhilaration. It is almost astonishing he did not suffer a massive heart attack and succumb on the spot. In all his wildest dreams and most sanguine hopes he had never imagined such a glorious day. His poetic soul, stirred beyond description, burst into a psalm of praise and honor and majesty to the Almighty that has seldom been matched in literature: *"Thine, O LORD, is the greatness and the*

*power, and the glory, and the victory, and the majesty:
for all that is in the heaven and in the earth is thine;
thine is the kingdom, O LORD, and thou art exalted as
head above all!"*

Human language is strained by such exaltation of spirit.
Our own spirits are stilled and quiet before the *living
God* as David pours out an unabashed stream of genuine
and profound gratitude for all that the Lord had done
for His people on this memorable occasion.

David had grasped clearly, as few ever do, that man
at best is but a pilgrim passing through the earthly scene.
We are here but briefly, at best our little lives no more
than a shifting shadow, a vanishing vapor that soon passes
into forgetfulness. Such acute awareness humbled him
as few great leaders have ever been humbled. He was
truly a man broken in heart, contrite in spirit who saw
with intense reality that everything a person possessed
came to him as a generous gift from a loving, caring God.
Humans are not self-made souls.

In this hour of such incredible ecstasy David did not
"strut his stuff" or congratulate himself as most public
figures would do. Quite the opposite! We see him bowed
before the Most High, giving to Him all the honor for
having so moved upon the hearts and wills of His people.
He protests in absolute sincerity that at best Israel was
only giving back some of the bounty God had bestowed
on her as a people.

It is a remarkable attitude of utter dependence on the
Lord! It rings so true! It is the heart-cry of a man who
above all else had set his will to do God's will. And from
my personal perspective as one who has now spent four
full years studying David's life, this was, without doubt,
his finest hour.

David's Abounding Joy Because of Israel's Generosity

His hymn of praise and prayer of supplication for his people transcend anything else which may have come from his soul by the inspiration of God's Spirit. In this his most majestic moment of triumph he utterly forgot himself. He was enveloped with an all-consuming passion that the attitude of his nation should always be this generous toward God, this amenable to His purposes, this willing to please Him.

But people were fickle, unpredictable, shifting with every changing wind of human pride.

So in anguish of heart and agony of spirit David implores God to preserve his son Solomon. How readily he could be tempted! How easily he could sin! How soon he could fall from favor with God!

Somehow with a profound spiritual perception, far beyond the ordinary, David sensed that his son would experience passionate spiritual struggles as his successor. Later events would prove the aged monarch to be correct. For, even though Solomon was later endowed with greater wisdom and more understanding than any other ruler, his reign was to end in folly and tragedy. No matter how great his concern for the good of the empire he had brought to preeminence, David simply could not guarantee its duration. Like every other civilization it would collapse in ruins because of human corruption within its society.

To the exuberant crowds on this special occasion such prospects may have seemed remote indeed. The empire was at its zenith. There was an aura of good will and elan such as Israel had not known in almost 450 years. Wealth and affluence were everywhere. A national desire to achieve great things gripped the people. Surely all was well. Or was it?

David now turned to his people once more with dignity and earnestness. *"Now, bless the LORD your God!"* he exhorted them.

God, very God, was their leader. He was really their true monarch. He was the source of their strength. He was the fountain of all their benefits. He was their protector and their salvation.

The huge assembly took David's instructions seriously. En masse they bowed themselves in humility and respect before the Most High. They worshiped with reverence just as massed crowds still do today in the Middle East where thousands prostrate themselves in the temple squares.

It is well to remind ourselves that all of this gigantic convocation was carried out without the benefit of public address systems or electronic amplifiers. So by the end of the long and historic occasion the aged king must have been almost at the end of his strength. His spiritual enthusiasm was the force which sustained his diminishing vitality. Never again would he appear in such splendor before his people.

The next day was given over to the appropriate offering of suitable sacrifices that were to atone for both the nation and for the king. These offerings were both sin offerings and peace offerings to the Lord Jehovah. They were done in accordance with the strict instructions of the high priests Zadok and Abiathar.

The slaughter of animals staggers us. One can only conclude that the huge numbers involved must have been deemed necessary to atone for all the diverse clans, families and leaders drawn together from every corner of the country. It may have seemed proper to engage in such massive sacrifices to be sure not a single segment of society was omitted. It could have been a very simple, human endeavor to be sure that any sin or wrong-doing committed by anyone in Israel had been completely atoned for.

One thousand steers were slaughtered.

One thousand choice rams were slain.

One thousand spotless lambs were sacrificed.

It stills our spirit and solemnizes our souls to realize that so much forfeiture of life, so much spilling of blood, was of absolutely no value or merit apart from its pure symbolism. For each death in itself was nothing more than a clear foreshadowing of the supreme sacrifice which God Himself would one day make in the perfect form of His own Son, the Lamb of God, slain from before the foundation of the world.

This David knew full well. He had spoken of it clearly in Psalm 22. Its great purpose was to bring peace between God and men on earth. And that was happening here (read carefully Hebrews 9).

Not only was the king concerned that all of Israel should be united as one nation, but even more so that they should be united with their God in a strong bond of love, loyalty and devotion to the Most High. For this to be so, there had to be total divine forgiveness and complete acceptance. The offerings and sacrifices were the ordained means to that ultimate end. They were not an orgy of bloodshed carried out in a primitive culture to indulge crude human debauchery. This needs to be understood clearly.

With the religious ordinances accomplished, the people themselves now sat down to celebrate the occasion with joyous festivities. Banquets were prepared and there was much merry-making amidst the spontaneous joy that engulfed the crowds and overflowed the entire royal city of Jerusalem.

A second time it was felt appropriate that the young Prince Solomon should be anointed with oil as a symbolic act of appointing him to the service of ruling God's chosen people. It was actually, now, his second coronation carried out in full view of all the assembled leaders of the nation.

He was assuming full responsibility for both the construction of the temple and the governing of God's people. In a remarkable act of genuine generosity David was relinquishing his own formidable authority and transferring it to his heir. It was a smooth and joyous transition. God was pleased that the prince of His choice had been brought to power.

Unhappily, despite the public support accorded to Solomon, there was afoot within the royal family a subversive element of discontent. Like a smouldering ember covered from view by a gray ash of respectability, it would erupt into flame before David's death. He would have to deal with it drastically. Even on David's deathbed the ultimate struggle for power would not yet be settled.

25

David Foils Adonijah's Insurrection

David had lived to be an aged monarch—a king greatly revered by his people, beloved for his music and poetry, respected for his remarkable wealth and power, famous far and wide for his military might, honored because of his great love and esteem for the Lord God.

Yet none of these notable achievements, either individually or combined, could or would exempt him from the final outworking of the great evil consequences of his illicit affair with Bath-sheba and the grim murder of her husband Uriah. Precisely as foretold by Nathan, violence and family feuds would follow the old gentleman to the end of his days.

Like so many elderly people, David, in the twilight of his years, lost condition physically. He became somewhat thin, feeble and unable to keep comfortably warm, especially in the winter months. It has often puzzled me why his physicians and personal advisers did not suggest that a second royal residence be established down at Jericho in the tropical surroundings of the warm Jordan valley. It would have been a sensible solution to his suffering.

Instead the rather outlandish suggestion was made that he be served, tended and cherished by the most lovely young maiden who could be found in his whole kingdom. Such an idea is rather typical of the mid-eastern mindset and represents the emphasis so often placed upon the purely physical aspect of human life. Perhaps David was too aged to reject this arrangement, or, on the other hand, he may have regarded it as a gesture of genuine love and concern for him by the nation in his declension.

In any event a beautiful girl from Shunam in the northern tribe of Isachaar was selected for this great honor. She must have been a teenager, perhaps only fourteen years of age, roughly sixty years younger than the wrinkled old monarch. To be expected to tend the personal and private needs of the ancient king with tender affection called for a lady of rare generosity and a gracious out-going spirit seldom found in one so young.

Abishag was her name, and until the time of David's death, she served as his closest companion and most intimate associate. However, he never took her as his wife, and any warmth she provided for the frail old king was much more of an emotional nature than the physical benefit her presence was intended to produce.

During this closing interlude of his life David appears to have lost touch with the affairs of state. This is of course quite understandable since much of the decision-making was now entrusted to his young coregent, Solomon. Perhaps out of deference and respect for the aged king, no one burdened him with day-to-day administration of the kingdom. Instead he was allowed to luxuriate softly in the genial company of the beautiful Abishag. No doubt there were those in Israel who felt strongly that David had served his people well and was now fully entitled to relax in semiretirement.

David Foils Adonijah's Insurrection

Whatever the reasons for the slackening in his rule, his fourth son, the rightful and legitimate remaining heir-apparent to the throne, Adonijah, took advantage of the situation. It will be recalled the oldest, first prince Amnon, was murdered in cold blood by David's third son Absalom. He in turn was murdered by Joab during the revolt against his father David. Scripture never discloses what happened to Daniel, David's second oldest son, born to lovely Abigail. One can only assume he, too, died. This meant that in truth Adonijah, the fourth prince, was in line for the throne.

But he, as well as all his brothers, had been by-passed in the selection of Solomon for the kingship. Not that this had been David's own decision. It was not. It was a divine decree that the king carried out carefully in accordance with the will of the Most High. There were great risks of rivalry involved despite David's appeal for unity and support from all his princes (sons).

Now during his indigence this rivalry erupted. Adonijah was determined to become king. With determination he set himself up, step by step, to succeed his father just exactly as Absalom had done. He, too, was a handsome, imposing person. He assembled horses and chariots for his own livery. He had formidable young footmen to run before him. He "strutted his stuff" and was daring enough to seek support from such venerable stalwarts as Joab, David's long time commander-in-chief, and Abiathar, the aged priest who had always served his father.

The stunning commentary of God's Word on all of this is that "not once had David ever crossed his son, nor attempted to correct his misconduct." As with Absalom, so with him. Adonijah was a totally spoiled young man. And one can only conclude he was capable of rallying public support to his claim for the throne because of the indigence of the leadership in the kingdom. For it was general knowledge that Solomon was to succeed David.

Without even trying to disguise his designs on the kingdom, Adonijah and his erstwhile supporters assembled at the Fuller's Spring, just outside the royal city, and held a full-fledged coronation banquet there. He was duly anointed with oil by Abiathar for his rule. He was shown public support by Joab who had prevailed on all the other princes, except Solomon, to attend the formal function. He was honored with a great feast at which the finest of fare and richest of wines were served. All of this culminated in a public coronation at which the great, ringing cry went up, *"God save King Adonijah!"*

Word of the "fait accompli" came back to Nathan the prophet. He was stunned by the news. Not only had he been omitted from the new monarch's guest list, but so also had Zadok, the king's other great high priest, and so had Benaiah, the commander of David's royal bodyguard. Why? Why had this insurrection taken place? Why had the clear instructions of God for the choice of Solomon as sovereign, suddenly been set aside? Why was Adonijah suddenly in power? Had the aged king changed his mind?

With his clear spiritual perception Nathan saw at once that the nation stood in peril. Two princes were now apparently in power, the older Adonijah having seized the sovereignty by right of inheritance. The younger Solomon had been put in power by divine decree. Who was to rule? Civil war and unbridled bloodshed could well be the only outcome of such a calamity. All David's dreams could crash in chaos.

Without a moment's delay the aged prophet went to see Bath-sheba the queen. Obviously she was a favorite with the king as well as a favorite in the royal court, even with her nephew Adonijah. She would be the only one who could resolve the issue quickly. He urged her to seek an audience with the king to tell him of the terrible threat to her son, Solomon's throne, and her own life. She alone could remind the monarch of his profound promises to her.

Bath-sheba moved as swiftly as a desert falcon stooping to defend its young. In moments she was in David's private quarters presenting her case, reminding his royal highness of his commitments to her and her son Solomon; demanding a decision that would determine the destiny of all Israel for all time.

No sooner had she spoken her piece, then Nathan stood outside the royal chambers, requesting an audience with the monarch. Ushered in by Abishag, while Bath-sheba went out, he repeated her report and quietly confirmed the crisis that had arisen. His main thrust was to determine if indeed the king, in his indigence, had changed his mind regarding a successor to the throne. For some obscure reason unknown to Nathan, had David decided to set Solomon aside after all? Or did Israel's monarch not know exactly what had transpired without his tacit approval?

A decision had to be made without delay!

To his monumental honor it must be declared that David was, to the end of his life, a man of action. He made some very regrettable decisions during his long reign, but he could act with firmness and finality. This was a case in point. Not for an instant did he hesitate; not for a moment did he debate the issues; not for a second did he allow the personal dangers to deter him. Amid his weakness and infirmity he still had a will of steel. He would use it to fulfill God's will no matter the catastrophic consequences.

Like a clean, cutting sweep of his battle sword, David ordered Bath-sheba back into his presence. All his private promises to her for Solomon to succeed him would be honored. It was God, very God, who had preserved and delivered him from every extremity. He would do so now again in sustaining her son on the throne and sparing the nation.

The queen, regal in her own robes, bowed herself to the floor beside his bed and blessed his name forever. His family, his kingdom, his dynasty would be perpetuated through their son Solomon.

She left the chambers while Nathan, who waited outside, was ushered in once more. But this time he was not alone. Already the king had sent off swift messengers to summon Zadok the high priest and Benaiah his chief officer of the royal guard. All three veteran counselors, who were national leaders, came in to stand before his majesty.

Propped up on his thick, embroidered pillows, his hands thin, boldly veined, trembling with age, David peered at the three gallant gentlemen through faded eyes. They must do his bidding. There was not a moment to lose. They were to be his feet, his hands, his eyes, his presence and his power. They would act on his behalf. They would carry out his commands, execute his authority.

He was still king in his kingdom.

He was still regent in the realm.

He was still shepherd over the sheep of Israel, wayward as they were, stupid as they seemed!

David was not about to vacate the throne again and flee the Royal City as he had done with Absalom. Under God's great hand he had been shown who should succeed him. The crucial hour had come when that succession should be implemented. There was not a moment to lose. He would foil Adonijah's designs.

With short, stabbing commands, sharp as angry sword thrusts, David issued his orders to the three aged stalwarts standing by his bed. They came swiftly in seven steps of sure succession. His enormous mental faculties were marshalled for this supreme moment of clean-cut decision.

1. Summon all his personal royal palace guard to arms.
2. Take Solomon and mount him on his own royal mule.
3. Parade in pomp to the great spring Gihon outside the walls.
4. There Zadok and Nathan should anoint him with oil.
5. Benaiah is to blow the coronation bugles.
6. All assembled shall shout, "God save King Solomon!"
7. He shall ride in honor into Jerusalem to ascend the throne.

All of the foregoing was to be accomplished because he, David, monarch over all the nation had personally appointed the young Solomon to rule over both Israel and Judah in his stead. The decision was made. The die was cast. The lot was drawn. There was no further discussion.

Valiant old Benaiah was so ecstatic over the king's action he could not restrain his emotions: *"Amen—so let it be!"* he exulted jubilantly. *"And may the LORD God himself say amen to this as well—granting Solomon even greater glory than his father!"*

Little did the fearless warrior realize how great a role he would play in seeing his own prayer fulfilled. He more than any other single person would be used to consolidate Solomon on the throne.

But for today, the three hurried away, intent only on carrying out David's immediate commands with the utmost alacrity.

The coronation ceremony, now the third for Solomon, shook the whole city with dazzling excitement. As is common with crowds the entire populace rushed off to join the royal parade with shouts of jubilation and the playing of flutes. The noise of the instruments, the stomping of military sandals on the sun-baked ground, the rising crescendo of singing and chanting shook the earth, rising like a mighty thunderstorm into the skies.

A new king had ascended the throne in Jerusalem!

Solomon sat in full-orbed splendor on his father's throne!

The royal succession had been accomplished in accord with the king's decree, in accordance with God's sovereign will!

The roar of the celebration, the blowing of the bugles, the sounds of jubilation rang through all of the Royal City. The uproar reached as far as the Fuller's Spring. There Adonijah, Joab, Abiathar and their handful of supporters were just finishing their presumptuous repast.

Immediately Joab was alarmed. His long experience as a battle commander alerted him at once to the ominous meaning of the distant thunderous applause. These sounds of singing and shouting made the hot blood in his old veins suddenly run cold. He had backed the wrong man! His future was frightening—and he was not normally a man given to fear of any foe.

At that very instant young Jonathan, the son of Abiathar the doddery old priest, who had double-crossed David in supporting Adonijah, came rushing into view. He was the same swift runner who had sped from Jerusalem to the Jordan to warn David to flee across the river from Absalom. He was one of the two youths who hid down in the well at Bahurim, and so was spared to save the king's life.

Here he came now to bring his father, and Adonijah, and Joab the devastating details of Solomon's coronation and ascension to David's throne. He had been in on the entire ceremony. And it may well have seemed incredulous to him that his father Abiathar would be so obtuse as to betray David in his old age and so support an impostor like Adonijah. All his life Abiathar had served David with such devotion, even in exile, why would he ever decide to abandon his friend now at the end of his illustrious life?

Jonathan described in detail how David, fallen back upon the ornate pillows of his royal bed, received the news of Solomon's ascension. Summoning the feeble resources of his failing strength the grand old monarch raised himself once more and bowed humbly in adulation before the Most High—*"Blessed be the LORD God of Israel,"* he declared clearly. *"He has spared me to see the day when the one of His choice would succeed me in power over His people!"*

It was enough! Like a covey of quail scattered to the four winds by the shot of a gun, all of Adonijah's fair weather friends flew off in different directions. Each was trying to survive in full flight from the explosive power of a new monarch in the realm.

In blind panic, Adonijah, suddenly a political refugee, rushed off to fling himself prostrate on the sacred horns of the altar in the tabernacle. It was the only place of refuge he could hope to survive Solomon's authority and revenge.

This news was brought to the fledgling king. His first royal act, recorded for us, is most revealing of the young man's self-restraint. *"If Adonijah shows himself worthy, he will suffer no harm. But if he is wicked, he will die,"* was the sinister warning sent back to the pretentious prince.

Adonijah, sure that he could survive, came and flung himself at Solomon's feet, bowing low, begging mercy. In his dark heart he was sure he could still unseat his younger brother.

Solomon's response was co-mingled constraint and wisdom. In compassion he decided to give Adonijah one more chance.

"Go home!" was his curt command. Only time would tell! Would he live or would he die?

26

David's Last Charge to Solomon and His Enduring Legacy

David's days drew to a close. His call "to go home" was at hand. He would not by-pass death in the rare and wondrous ways accorded Enoch, Moses or Elijah. He was destined to die as most of us are. He would have to walk through the valley of the shadow of death about which he had written so poignantly in Psalm 23. This he could do with great dignity and quiet assurance because he would pass through the portals of eternity in company with the great Shepherd of his soul.

For the child of God, death is not a dread. It is but the doorway through which we step from this earthly dimension of time, space and brief mortality into the glorious dimension of eternity, and life everlasting. It is to be set free from sin, sorrow, sickness and the despair of earth into the spectacular freedom of liberty in the life and light and love of the Most High who makes heaven, our home, a realm of magnificent repose. What hope, what expectation, what assurance the Lord gives those who rest in His preparations for them!

All of this David knew with sure and unshakable confidence. His own personal hope was in the Most High. His calm confidence rested in the impeccable character of the Almighty whom he longed to see in person—as he put it so beautifully in Psalm 17: *"As for me, I will behold Thy face in righteousness: I shall be satisfied when I awake, with Thy likeness."*

No, David had no dread of the future. He had unshakable faith in the ultimate goodness of his Lord God. And that solid, spiritual assurance has become a profound part of the enduring legacy which he left to all of us. Few indeed are the great men of God who have equaled him in sharing quiet trust with those who came after. It is without question the finest contribution he ever made to the community of man.

But before his own departure to be with the Lord, the aged monarch was acutely concerned for the on-going well-being of both his heir to the throne and his empire. David had no personal dread of death. Yet he entertained a profound dread of the diabolical devices of those who might destroy Solomon and his dynasty. He himself had been delivered again and again from destruction by the mighty hand of the Most High. Somehow he was not sure Solomon would survive in the same manner.

So the young king was summoned to his father's bedside for a last charge before the living God. The sage advice he would be given was both spiritual and practical.

First of all David restated the bedrock truths which alone could sustain the youthful monarch amid all of his adversities—and which apply equally to each of us. Here they are in condensed form:

1. Keep the charge of the Lord to live uprightly.
2. Walk humbly in the paths of righteousness.
3. Obey God's edicts and commandments.

4. Love His law and be loyal to His desires.
> This was the secret to success.
> This was the path to prosperity.
> This was the way to honor and repose.

Once again with great fervency of spirit, using all the physical energy he could muster, David assured his son that only in this way could he expect to be blessed by the Lord. This was his part of the covenant to carry out before the Almighty. There was no other way in which he could count on God to fulfill all of His promises to his father David.

In short, Solomon was reminded for a last time that it was expected of him to live a life of integrity, loyalty and truth both before his people and before his God.

If he would honor the Almighty, his kingdom would endure.

Then, almost as an afterthought, David felt he should impress on his young son several important practical steps he should take to protect himself and the empire. In the record given to us they convey the first impression of being an act of revenge. But David was not a vindictive person! All through his illustrious life he had demonstrated an unusual capacity to forgive those who had wronged him. It was one of his most admirable attributes.

What he was doing here was warning Solomon to guard himself zealously against men like Joab and Shimei. These were individuals who could do both him and the empire enormous damage if left unchecked.

All during his career David had great difficulty with Joab. The ferocious general had murdered not only Abner and Amasa, his rivals, in cold blood, but even David's son Absalom in the heat of battle. He had joined Adonijah in his conspiracy to usurp the throne. So who knew what other devious designs he might have upon the empire? He simply had to be dealt with drastically.

David also reminded Solomon that Shimei was another contriving individual who simply could not be trusted. The king had taken more verbal abuse and insults from this malignant man from Bahurim than anyone else in his life. It was altogether possible he might again rise up in rebellion against the throne. So he too needed to be kept under the closest surveillance.

Finally in a most moving manner, the feeble old king, now lying exhausted in his royal chambers, reminded Solomon of the great kindness Barzillai had shown him. When David fled in fear across the Jordan from the angry uprising of his own son Absalom, it was the fierce old desert chief who had given him shelter and supplies.

Now in turn Solomon was to bestow on Barzillai's sons the honor of dining at his royal table. They should be given the same kindness he had given to Mephibosheth, Jonathan's crippled son.

These practical steps, simple, stern and severe as they were, would go far to consolidate Solomon's hold on the throne. His reputation as a powerful ruler would spread rapidly. His wisdom and understanding in dealing with difficult individuals would be demonstrated dramatically.

Then David died!

We are given no details of the great state funeral which he must have been accorded by his devoted nation.

The simple statements are made in stark truth that:
he ruled Judah in Hebron for seven years;
he ruled all of Israel in Jerusalem thirty-three years;
he died in a good old age, full of days;
he ended his career with enormous wealth;
he enjoyed great honor at the end of his reign.

It is a plain yet powerful tribute to a king whose roots

were in the warm pasture lands of the sheep ranges out-side Bethlehem. It is the sort of stark yet regal epitaph given to a man whose single, yet greatest purpose in life was *"to do God's will."*

The accolades given to him by both his contemporaries and later historians do not really do him justice. For a proper appraisal of his true character and unique career we must discover what God's estimation was of this indi-vidual. That verdict is much more significant than any-thing men might say, write or think.

We find the appraisal made by God in three subsequent revelations in which the Most High spoke very clearly to Solomon about his father David. To put these in proper orderly sequence we must follow Solomon's career briefly for a few more years. Only then will we see that David's death did not mark the end of David's impact on the empire he had built.

He did not just pass into oblivion. He was not just forgot-ten like another leaf fallen to the ground. His fame, his influence, his devotion to God would endure as an inspira-tion to his succeeding generations. He was Israel's great-est king!

Swiftly, surely, Solomon took severe steps to show the nation he was truly a successor to his father David. He would brook no rivals. He would tolerate no one not true to the throne.

His first drastic action was to dispose of Adonijah. No sooner had David died, then Adonijah decided to have another try for the throne. He approached Bath-sheba to have her request the right for him to take Abishag, the beautiful young lady who had cared for David. To ask for her hand was a subtle and insidious scheme to seek the preeminence in power. It was a crafty move that enraged Solomon. Immediately he ordered Benaiah,

241

his chief of the royal guard, to go over and liquidate Adonijah on the spot.

Adonijah had been given the chance to go home and live in peace. Instead he chose to play his subtle games. So death was the consequence, exactly as Solomon had warned him.

The second swift move the new king made was to depose Abiathar the high priest, at once. Solomon knew of his intrigue and open support for Adonijah. Had the ancient, toothless man not been so loyal to David most of his life, he, too, would have been slain on the spot. Still Solomon would have none of his nonsense. He was sent back to his home, banished into oblivion the rest of his days.

Hearing of Solomon's terrifying tactics, Joab knew there was not a hope in the new realm for him. He had played his hand wrongly in backing Adonijah for the throne.

In stark terror he, too, fled to the tabernacle flinging himself on the horns of the altar hoping for a reprieve. But it was not to be! When he refused to leave the sanctuary, Benaiah was sent to dispatch him there. So he fell like an overripe fruit that had rotted on the branch of his family tree.

Shimei, too, was put to the sword by the strong arm of Benaiah for refusing to comply with Solomon's command, that he be confined to his home in Jerusalem.

In stern succession all of Solomon's erstwhile rivals and possible foes were eliminated from the public life of the nation. No longer would he have to delegate his time or attention to the sort of insurgency that had plagued his father, David. He had sent a strong, clear, unmistakable signal to the entire empire that though he was young, he was mature in wisdom and mighty in understanding the wicked ways of men.

With the same undivided devotion that David had shown to the Lord God, Solomon set about his duty to erect the temple. His father had built a mighty empire to the honor of the Most High. He would build a magnificent edifice to the glory of God.

He simply could not do this with his own skill or using his own strength. He needed the same sort of divine direction that David his father had received from the Almighty.

In his compassion and loving concern for the fledgling king, God appeared to him in a dream by night. The story is well known, the account clearly documented for us by the Spirit of God. In the night vision Solomon is offered whatever supernatural help he might need.

In his humility of heart the young monarch beseeches God to bestow on him divine wisdom and supernatural understanding to rule Israel aright. God is so pleased He grants him this request as well as the promise of enormous wealth, honor and riches surpassing those ever known before.

Then there was added a proviso most people forget: *"If you will walk in My ways and keep My commandments as your father David did, I God, very God, will lengthen your days!"* (*1 Kings 3:14*).

This was God's estimation of David's life. It had set a standard of supreme consecration by which Solomon would be measured. From God's perspective David had lived a superb life.

For seven years after David's death, the construction of the magnificent temple went on steadily. At long last the final cedar board was covered in gold leaf; the very last beautiful furnishing was crafted; the most precious stone of ornamentation glowed in its appointed place.

There remained now only the glory of God, the effulgence of His presence, the power of His might, to fill this sacred sanctuary. It would be the culmination of the national dream. It would be the fulfillment of David's deepest desire.

Again a second time the Lord God appeared to Solomon just as He had the first time. He assured him that He, the Most High, had hallowed this sanctuary and that His presence would be pleased to reside there among His people. Then, wonder of wonders, He declared emphatically to Solomon exactly how highly He esteemed David—how he was a man of incredible integrity and uprightness in heart.

> *"And if thou wilt walk before me,*
> *as David thy father walked, in integrity of heart,*
> *and in uprightness, to do according to all that*
> *I have commanded thee, and wilt keep My statutes*
> *and My judgments:*
> *Then I will establish the throne of thy kingdom*
> *upon Israel forever, as I promised to David*
> *thy father, saying, there shall not fail thee*
> *a man upon the throne of Israel"* (1 Kings 9:4–5).

All of Solomon's glory, all of his power, all of his dynasty depended upon conduct and character of David's caliber. What a superb accolade and tribute from God Himself!

Finally on that monumental occasion when Jehovah was pleased to come down upon the Royal City and occupy the temple, He again spoke to Solomon in person about David. That day the magnificence of His divine splendor had filled the sanctuary. The celestial fire of

His supernatural presence had consumed the sacrifices on the altar. The Eternal One had come to dwell in power amongst His people (2 Chronicles 7).

A third time the Most High reminded Solomon that amid all the excitement of this majestic occasion David had not been forgotten. It was this humble, gifted, great Shepherd King who had lived before Him in utter faithfulness.

At the very outset of David's public life God had declared through Samuel, *"The LORD seeth not as man seeth: for man looketh on the outward appearance, but the LORD looketh on the heart."* Now after the close of the king's illustrious career the Most High declared unequivocally: *"David walked before Me in integrity of heart!"*

If he, Solomon, would do likewise his kingdom would endure. And the covenant He made with David would endure. It was the grandest eulogy any mortal had ever been given by God.

27

Reflections: Basic Spiritual Truths Brought Out in This Book

In all the circumstances of life we should seek clear guidance from God. We need to be specific and know His will even in the small decisions.

One of the hallmarks of God's child is the capacity to forgive others for their wrongs. This is clear evidence that we have experienced the gracious forgiveness of Christ ourselves.

Brutality and violence are very much a part of unregenerate human nature. A Christian who honors the Lord does not indulge in such pursuits for pleasure.

To resist God's will is to invite disaster. To ignore His instructions is to court certain ruin.

Those who trust the Most High to direct their affairs often have to wait long and patiently for Him to accomplish His work behind the scenes. He is not always in a great hurry as we are.

Reflections: Basic Spiritual Truths in This Book

Faith in God requires boldness to state our desires, unshakable confidence in the trustworthiness of our Father, a willingness to wait for Him to fulfill our needs.

The person who produces peace in this world is in truth a child of God.

Our Father uses difficult people in our lives to conform us to His own character and to drive us to seek His solace.

We live in a world conditioned by death. So we must ever live ready to die. Are we ready for "the call home"?

It is the Lord who calls each of us to serve Him and His purposes in the world. This we do gladly to please Him and to be a benefit to our generation, not to exalt ourselves!

Part of this service is to enter into the sufferings of others. To share their sorrow, sickness and sadness as Christ did.

One of the foremost priorities for God's people is to give God's Word great honor. It is the expression of His will for us. It calls for our hearty compliance. When this is done His gracious benefits are bestowed.

It is exceedingly dangerous to despise another person. God loves them just as He loves me. This is often forgotten.

Sometimes our Father's answer to our requests is a denial. This does not infer He does not care. He alone knows best.

The profound awareness, *"O God, You know me. You alone fully understand me,"* is a Christian's great consolation. On this basis he allows the Lord to occupy all of his life gladly. In this way we become true temples of residence for the Most High.

It is imperative that God's people honor their commitments to Him and to each other. Our word should be an emblem of fidelity and credibility.

There is enormous good in helping those who cannot reciprocate. This self-losing action demonstrates the genuine love of God.

Our minds, imaginations and emotions, unless controlled by Christ, can be monsters that manipulate us and lead us into great evil. Things are not always as they appear. With spiritual perception we can see things from God's perspective.

Because of living by faith we can be brave for the Lord.

No man or woman sins alone. The wrong is a crime against God and against others; and it can mean destruction of ourselves. Thereby we forfeit peace with God, the esteem of others and our own self-respect. The way of the sinner is hard!

One misdeed, unless confessed and repented of, inevitably leads to another in rapid succession. The pit of wrongdoing grows ever deeper. Only turning to God in contrition can extricate a man from the mire. The ultimate choice is ours: which will we have, death—or life in Christ?

Because of the inviolate nature of our Father's commands, the consequences of sin are serious. We reap what we sow in life. God's gracious pardon can remove the guilt and the grime of our wrongs, but the error of our ways will be felt to the end of our days.

Genuine godly repentance before the Lord is the sure path to peace with Him and good will among men.

The amazing grace of our merciful Lord is beyond human comprehension. He will pick up, restore and remake anyone who in utter sincerity casts themselves upon His mercy. His love far transcends anything known among men.

It is at great peril that God's person forms any close or intimate association with a non-Christian.

God-fearing parents should be bold enough to discipline their children and instruct them in the paths of righteousness. This may cause alienation, but God will bring good out of it.

It is when Christians are timid that the worldlings become brave and arrogant. Too often God's people give tacit approval to evil by their silence.

There is such a thing as false forgiveness, an easy tolerance, which nourishes the seeds of crimes committed.

The very integrity and righteousness of God demands that justice be done. Likewise in our lives the same must be true. Mercy and justice complement each other.

249

The use of violence or terror to achieve one's ends is despicable. It is invariably accompanied by intrigue and deception.

God, our Father, can use the most grievous experiences of our lives to shape our characters. And, if we will but allow Him to He can bring great good out of our distress.

True worship of the Most High is more than mere words. It means *I acknowledge God is God* in every event. It means *I accept* His arrangement of my affairs. It means that *I approve* heartily of any means He uses to manage my life.

It is because our Father loves us so profoundly and cares so deeply for our welfare that He disciplines us. At the time it may seem traumatic. But the grief leads to godliness.

Christians in positions of leadership should be bold for God, willing to risk much for the honor of His name.

The Lord is here. He is alive, active, at work in the world. Because of this He often surprises us with sudden and quite unexpected answers to our prayers. He can bring great benefits out of what appear to us, sometimes, as great evil! So trust Him totally.

Meekness is not weakness. It is the mark of an approachable person prepared to cooperate with God and man in doing what is fine and noble.

We should never allow our own sorrows or problems to so dominate our lives that we become oblivious to the suffering of others around us. This is self-centeredness of the worst sort. Every person bears some private burden.

Too many parents have "tunnel vision" with respect to their own offspring. They wear "blinders" to their misdeeds. They indulge their misconduct. This is a great evil.

It is a truly great person who is generous enough to his enemies to forgive their wrongs and overlook their faults, when he is in a position to punish them. Jesus said this is proof we are God's children.

We live in a world where rivalry, duplicity and intrigue are the warp and woof of social behavior. All of this is a great weariness to Christ. It should be to us as well. We should have no part in it.

Jealousy and envy are destructive evils in the family of God. Those who foster division and discord bring serious consequences on themselves and others.

The most ordinary person, when living by faith in the Lord, can be used by Him to perform exploits.

Those in positions of leadership need to set an example of being people of integrity, fidelity and loyalty. These elements are becoming scarce in society.

Both in national and private life there is a need for repentance from wrong, a humbling of ourselves, a turning to seek God's face, a desire to do His will in love.

We dare not forsake our Father if we wish to prosper in peace.

The Most High is our rock, our fortress, our deliverer, our refuge, our shield, our horn, our *Savior . . . not men!*

Ultimately our confidence should repose in the power of Christ not in the wisdom or expertise of human beings.

God does not look for perfect people to achieve His work in the world. There are none! Nor does He prefer to choose gifted individuals. More often than not they are too proud to be usable.

Rather, the truth is, our Father looks for certain specific qualities not readily ascertained by outward human observation:

1. Total availability to whatever He wishes.
2. A willingness to do His Will, even if it costs suffering.
3. Genuine humility of spirit ready to repent of wrong.
4. A generous attitude that puts all we possess at the disposal of His purposes.

Such persons are few and far between, perhaps less than two percent in the church world-wide.

The impact of a person's life on others, for the honor of the Most High, is directly dependent on the degree to which the Lord lives in that individual day by day. Christ calls us to deny ourselves daily in order to do His bidding daily. He must be in command. For most this is too high a price to pay.

Modern man, like men of old, rely on human resources. Yet God's Spirit ever calls us to rely on God. The choice is ours. We are, each of us, the sum total of all our choices.

The Almighty will move the earth or shift the sun to touch any common man or woman who will just do His Will. He will bless beyond measure anyone who in love and loyalty gives Him all they own.

On what do we fasten our affection? The world or God?

Collectively the people of God (the Church) are His residence on earth. But so are we each as individuals, the Royal Residence of the Most High. What an honor! In it day and night may continuous praise rise to the Almighty!

It matters not whether one be small or great, skilled or unskilled, the Lord can use that person to achieve much.

God will endow the person available to Him with very special gifts and abilities to do His beautiful work in the world. This is possible because it is He who is here with us to do it.

Any group, church or nation will go only as far as their leader has gone with God. He sets the example for his people.

All wealth, power and intelligence come from God our Father as gifts. Anything we possess is really His! Let Him have it. Only what we share with others in love and compassion ever counts in the accounts of eternity.

253

Only the Almighty truly knows and sees our inner motives. Our deepest desires should be to please Him and bless others.

As age advances, God's child is constrained more and more to find his strength and solace in Christ. The life needs to be in order, ready for the call home. Looking back across the years we see clearly, *"It is God who always delivered me!"*

We are put on earth *"to know God: to love Christ: to enjoy the company of His Spirit: to do His will: to enrich others."* Not to serve ourselves!

In the end, it is God's estimation of us that counts—not man's!